AT HOME IN THE COTSWOLDS

SECRETS OF ENGLISH COUNTRY HOUSE STYLE

KATY CAMPBELL *and* MILO CAMPBELL

Photographs by MARK NICHOLSON

ABRAMS, NEW YORK

CONTENTS

Foreword by the Duchess of Marlborough 7
The Cotswolds—an Introduction 11

THE HOUSES

The Manor House 25
The Thatched Cottage 37
The Columbarium 49
The Mason's House 65
The Old Rectory 77
The "Hovel" 91
The High House 103
The Farm Worker's Cottage 115
The Arts and Crafts House 127
The Dovecote 141
The Georgian Farmhouse 153
The Village House 165
The Hotchpotch 177
Cottage Industry 189
The Stately Home 201
Paradise 217

About the Homeowners 231
Acknowledgements 235
Index 236

FOREWORD
by the Duchess of Marlborough

*H*aving been brought up in South Wales I sometimes like to tease my husband by saying that I find the Cotswolds a bit flat. But over the years I've come to love the gently sloping hills and undulating landscape of these wolds as much as he.

Blenheim Palace sits at the eastern point of the Cotswolds Area of Outstanding Natural Beauty and is a place of extraordinary beauty itself. It was built as Queen Anne's gift to John Churchill, 1st Duke of Marlborough, in gratitude for his military campaigning and defeat of Louis XIV in 1704. Sir John Vanbrugh's baroque masterpiece is the only non-royal or episcopal building in Britain that is labelled a palace, and most would agree that it lives up to that moniker on scale alone.

It is an enormous privilege to live in this part of the world and to enjoy the beauty of the palace and park. Our most favourite things are early morning walks with the dogs through the ancient oak woods and family rides with the children through the park.

The Duke and I divide our time between the palace and a farmhouse on the estate where I have a kiln and work on my pots *[The Duchess is a ceramicist who trained at the Royal College of Art]*. We love staying at Blenheim with our family and friends as despite its grandeur the private apartments are surprisingly cosy. And there is always something exciting going on, like the Salon Privé, music concerts, or Giffords Circus—a particular favourite of the children—to name but a few.

Many of my friends also live in the Cotswolds, some of whose houses are featured in this wonderful book. Much of the architecture of the region is fashioned out of the same honeyed stone that was used to build Blenheim.

PREVIOUS PAGE: The south façade of Blenheim Palace

ABOVE: The Great Court and front entrance to the palace

OPPOSITE: The Duchess with two of her dogs, Midge and Mouse, at Blenheim Palace. She is sitting at a George III Carlton House writing desk (c.1800) in the room known as "the Duchess's Sitting Room." On the desk, next to family photographs, is a jug made by the Duchess herself.

I was recently introduced to this poem, written by Hilaire Belloc, about the River Evenlode, which runs from Moreton-in-Marsh to the Thames and passes through Blenheim Park on its way:

> The Tender Evenlode that makes
> Her meadows hush to hear the sound
> Of waters mingling in the brakes,
> And binds my heart to English ground.
>
> A lonely river, all alone,
> She lingers in the hills and holds,
> A hundred little towns of stone,
> Forgotten in the western wolds.

It reminds me how lucky I am to be surrounded by such beauty and, despite my Welsh roots, how my heart is very much bound to this most quintessential of English landscapes.

—*Edla Marlborough, Duchess of Marlborough*

THE COTSWOLDS— AN INTRODUCTION

If you open a British passport and look inside the front cover, you will find a picture of a group of picturesque cottages. They are located in Bibury, described by William Morris as "the most beautiful village in England." And Bibury itself is located in that most iconic of all British landscapes—the Cotswolds. This image, tucked away in the breast pocket of every Briton travelling abroad, is fitting because there are few things more quintessentially British, nor closer to the national heart, than the dream of a perfect Cotswold house.

The Cotswolds is an Area of Outstanding Natural Beauty (AONB) covering 800 square miles and crossing five counties. It is named for the gently undulating folds in its verdant landscape and is famous for its river valleys, historic market towns, stone-built villages, and ancient beech woods. It is home to artists, writers, rock stars, and royalty. And thanks, in part, to the popularity of films and TV shows such as *Bridget Jones's Diary*, *Downton Abbey*, and *Pride and Prejudice*, its charming cottages and grand country houses have grabbed the imagination of a global audience. Internationally recognised as one of the most beautiful places on earth, the Cotswolds attracts more than 38 million visitors every year.

This popularity is not a recent phenomenon. The Cotswolds has always drawn mankind to its environs. Neolithic long barrows and standing stones and the remains of ancient hill forts can be found littered throughout the area. This plethora of prehistoric sites speaks of the hold these rolling hills had on early men and women. And the Cotswolds' popularity continued through the ages. When the ancient Romans conquered Britain in the first century AD, they quickly determined that this peaceful place of beauty provided the perfect antidote to the bustle of Londinium and built their country villas here. A vogue that has continued to this day.

Two things more than anything else are responsible for the elevation of this landscape from pretty countryside to one of the most enchanting places on earth—a type of rock and a breed of sheep.

OPPOSITE: The world-famous Arlington Row in Bibury. These seventeenth-century weavers' cottages were created from a monastic wool store built in 1380.

The rock in question was formed during the Jurassic era when this part of the world was submerged beneath a tropical sea teeming with marine reptiles, prehistoric crustaceans, and ammonites the size of bicycle wheels. The coral reefs of these shallow waters gradually became covered by silt and clay and over the next 200 million years hardened into an oolitic limestone, named after the egg-like granules from which it is composed. Eventually the oceans receded, the world ceased to tremble under the feet of dinosaurs, and this wondrous limestone remained, lying just a few inches below the surface of the earth.

Because of its abundance and its relative softness, which makes it easy to work with, this marvellous stone became the dominant building material in the Cotswolds from the Middle Ages onwards. Everything in the area is built from it. It is used for dry stone walls, for the rubble of cottages, in ashlar cut blocks for smartly appointed manor houses, and for the stone tiles on roofs, and is carved into magnificent arches, traceries, and finials in the region's churches. Buff, cream, honey, or gold, it ranges in colour and tone as one traverses the Cotswolds. And it takes on an almost magical lustre when lit by the sun.

As if the landscape were not picturesque enough, wherever you go in the Cotswolds you will see flocks of sheep artfully scattered across its fields, like table decorations. The Romans farmed them first and the Anglo-Saxons took the practice on, setting them to graze in enclosures called "cots," which gives us a literal translation for the Cotswolds—"sheep hills." Cotswold sheep are calm and friendly, and their rams are without horns. Yet despite their gentle demeanour the breed is known as "the Cotswold Lion" because of their stature and importance. Their wool is long, soft, glossy, and strong. It is also slightly golden in colour. This luxurious product has always been highly prized. Florentine merchants as far back as the thirteenth century would travel to England specifically to buy large quantities of this highly prized wool. They would weave it with fine strands of real gold to make the fabled "cloth of gold" worn by kings and priests in the Middle Ages. The success of the woollen trade brought immense wealth to the Cotswolds. Farmers and wool merchants amassed great fortunes on the back of these noble sheep—fortunes that were converted into stone as they built grand manor houses for themselves, alongside barns, farmhouses, and cottages for their workers. The philanthropic amongst them also built schools, almshouses, and, most importantly, churches.

A particularly fine example of these medieval "wool churches" can be found within my hometown of Fairford, on the banks of the River Coln. St. Mary's was built in the late fifteenth century by a local wool merchant named John Tame. He must have been fabulously wealthy as the church he commissioned, in what is still today a very modestly sized town, is lavish in its exquisite stonework and

LEFT: Burford's Sheep Street. This ancient market town is known as the Gateway to the Cotswolds.

BELOW: The River Windrush with the steeple of St. John the Baptist's Church, Burford, beyond.

LEFT: An eighteenth-century folly in the Deer Park of Great Barrington Park

ABOVE. A typical Cotswold beech wood carpeted with bluebells

decoration. It was specially designed to house a set of twenty-eight stained glass windows whose quality rivalled that of the great European cathedrals of the time (and, remarkably, that glass remains to this day). Tame would have been the equivalent of a contemporary hedge fund billionaire filling his house with Rothkos and Picassos.

The legacy of this geological blessing of stone, combined with the golden fleece of the Cotswold Lion, is a collection of buildings that we seek to celebrate in this book. Buildings that range in size and style from the humblest farm workers' dwellings to the most resplendent of aristocratic palaces, and all manner of property in between. If you climb to a high point anywhere in the Cotswolds and look out over the valleys below, you cannot fail to spot a glorious manor house in the distance, or a whisp of smoke rising from the chimney of a lodge, or glimpse the stone tiled roof of an old rectory beyond a church spire—all of them nestled organically into the landscape and built from the same honeyed stone upon which they sit.

There are some famous pockets within the AONB: "Royal Gloucestershire" around Tetbury and Badminton, where the Prince of Wales, the Princess Royal, and other members of the family have made their home; the steep valleys of "Laurie Lee Country" around Stroud; the uber-fashionable villages of "Daylesfordshire" (which centre around the upmarket farm shop of that name), and the exquisite architecture to be found in the tourist towns of the North Cotswolds where you will find the likes of Chipping Campden and Broadway. The region is crossed by rivers like the Windrush, the Evenlode, and the Churn, whose waters teem with trout, otters, and water voles. And dotted around are ancient woodlands and forests, which are home to foxes, deer, badgers, and rhinoceroses. (Although in fairness the rhinos are mostly to be found grazing on the lawns in front of the strawberry gothic manor house of the Cotswold Wildlife Park, near Burford.)

The homes in this book are scattered throughout the region. They are all of different sizes and built in a range of architectural manners. Their owners are a diverse group, each of whom has imposed their own taste and style upon their houses. All are united, however, in creating glorious idylls for themselves in this most captivating of pastoral landscapes.

OPPOSITE, TOP AND BOTTOM: Dry stone walls built from Cotswold stone

OVERLEAF: The tower of the Church of St. Andrew in Miserden, which dates back to the thirteenth century

ABOVE: A western Cotswolds view

TOP RIGHT: Little Barrington

RIGHT: Miserden valley

The HOUSES

The Manor House

There has been a house on the site of Fyfield Manor since time immemorial, as evidenced by the Roman well in the garden, the Saxon bridge at the bottom of the meadow, and the half basement under the house that historians date as pre–tenth century. It's not hard to understand why. The plot sits above a gently meandering section of the River Leach whose silvery waters flow into the Thames by the village of Buscot some five miles further south. It is an idyllic setting on the edge of the village of Southrop—famous for its tiny Norman church, within whose herringbone-patterned stone walls local resident Kate Moss married her rock guitarist husband.

The house, as it stands today, is a perfect small manor house with an exceptionally pretty, symmetrical façade that dates back to the 1720s. David Verey, in Pevsner's *Buildings of England*, describes Fyfield, with typical understatement, as "a rather elegant little house." I would go further than Verey. I think it an exquisite example of early Georgian architecture. And I am not alone. When it last came onto the market five years ago, more than three hundred people viewed it and a bidding war ensued. The eventual winners were the interior designer Joanna Wood and her husband, Charles Hansard. Charles had spotted it first. They had been looking for a house in the southern part of the Cotswolds, but even though Fyfield Manor was out of their search area, he convinced Joanna that "it was too pretty not to view." He was correct. Joanna fell in love immediately—"It was like something straight out of a Jane Austen novel"—and she knew instantly that it was the perfect house for their family.

The front of the house originally consisted of a central hall with a parlour on either side. This is now an elegant drawing room with a study off it. Behind this is a hallway with a dog-leg staircase leading to the first floor. Here, in what was originally the *piano nobile*, is the main bedroom, in a projected bay with windows on three sides. Joanna's bathroom sits in what would have been "the withdrawing room" off it. On the other side is Charles's dressing room. Guest bedrooms are found in the floor above, under the gabled roof with its ancient Cotswold stone tiles and ball finials on the parapets. Beyond these main rooms of the eighteenth-century façade are the earlier parts of the house that extend along two wings.

OPPOSITE: Fyfield Manor's early Georgian façade

OPPOSITE: Hanging above the AGA oven is Joanna's collection of vintage leaf-patterned plates. Above the island is an unusual "Vertigo" pendant light. The rest of the family were unsure about it when Joanna first bought it. "Charles complained that it looks like a giant Ascot hat! But just two weeks later it was selected by the V&A as a design classic of the future, and I was vindicated and now they love it."

It took Joanna a year to get planning permission on her vision to connect the two wings of the landmark (Grade II listed) house with a new front hall and turn what was originally a dairy into her kitchen. She employed Oxfordshire-based architects Johnston Cave to design the generous single-storey hallway with its Buscot stone floor and the redesigned rooms beyond. It took a further two and a half years to finish the house to her exacting standards (and the gardens remain "a work in progress").

It was the society tastemaker Nancy Lancaster, from her Cotswold base of Ditchley Park, who first distilled what has come to be known as the English country house style. From the 1940s onwards, when she bought the legendary interior decorating firm Colefax and Fowler, Lancaster was responsible for spreading this quintessential look. Joanna Wood is both a fan and a leading exponent of this style. It is a look that she has provided for many of her clients over the years (including, recently, for the US ambassador at Winfield House in London), and it is one that she has adopted at Fyfield Manor. As she points out, English country house style is never out of fashion. It is, by its nature, timeless, and as one can see with the likes of the uber-trendy Mayfair club 5 Hertford Street, it is as popular as ever. At its heart it involves floral linens and chintzes, a willingness to embrace colour, and a mixture of antique furniture (that is not beholden to one period). The look is formal but relaxed with an abundance of cushions, rugs, books, flowers, and *objets* that soften the edges of what are often grand reception rooms.

The house and garden now provide the perfect base for an enviable life in the country. The main house contains six bedrooms (one includes Charles's dressing room, "which he is not inclined to give over to guests unless a very special occasion dictates"). A stable cottage across the front drive provides two additional bedrooms for shooting parties and tennis weekends. The family makes particular use of the swimming pool with its hidden changing room cut into the centre of a yew hedge. Joanna has also used hedging to hide the tennis court from view and has cleverly used the earth removed to create it to build what looks like a prehistoric burial mound. It offers an ideal spot for picnics and for taking in the pastoral views down to the river.

The gardens include a productive orchard from which Joanna produces her own label apple juice to give to friends and family. And her latest project is honey making, with a newly installed hive where she hopes the bees will feed off the wildflowers in the meadow beyond. There is no doubt about it, centuries after its first inhabitants arrived, life at Fyfield Manor continues to be idyllic.

OPPOSITE: The fireplace in the drawing room is original, as is the panelling. It is pine, as Georgians always painted over it (only very grand houses had oak). Joanna has drag painted it in three shades of white—a nineteenth-century technique that brings warmth and softness to the room.

ABOVE LEFT: An Aubusson rug in the bay dictated the colour scheme for the room. There is a mixture of antique furniture, some inherited (like Joanna's mother's card table—"she was terrifyingly good at bridge"), some part of a lifetime spent prowling antiques shops and auction houses with her magpie eye, and some belonging to the previous occupants of Fyfield and bought in the sale of contents alongside the house.

ABOVE RIGHT: Gypsy, Joanna's border terrier, at the side door to the hall

The study is painted in the amusingly named Very Well Red by Paint and Paper Library. Over the fireplace is a portrait of Joanna in her early twenties painted by Sue Ryder (who also, famously, painted Princess Diana in her wedding dress).

ABOVE: The linens in the main bedroom are all by Lewis and Wood—the fabric and wallpaper company co-founded by Joanna.

RIGHT: Guest bedrooms are found under the gabled roof, with its ancient Cotswold stone tiles and ball finials on the parapets.

OPPOSITE: The wonderfully light marble-floored main bathroom has Indienne Tint wallpaper by Lewis and Wood, to match the curtains and blinds in the main bedroom.

RIGHT AND BELOW: The gardens include a productive orchard and a newly installed hive, where bees can feed on the wildflowers in the meadow beyond.

ABOVE: The swimming pool has a hidden changing room cut into the centre of a yew hedge, which also hides the tennis court from view.

The Thatched Cottage

*F*irst things first: This is NOT the cottage from *The Holiday*. In case you are unfamiliar with the film, *The Holiday* is a cult romantic comedy about two love-lorn women on either side of the Atlantic doing a house swap over Christmas. In it, Cameron Diaz swaps her LA house for Kate Winslet's rustic cottage in the English countryside. A cottage that looks remarkably like the one owned by designer Bee Osborn. "I had never heard of the film, but one day I took a photo of my cottage in the snow and posted it on Instagram. It went completely viral, with thousands of people commenting that it was the one from *The Holiday*. Eventually my daughter sat me down and made me watch the film." The actual cottage in the film, where Diaz falls in love with Jude Law, is a fake—a specially built shell that was constructed in a field near Shere in Surrey, with its interiors created on a sound stage in Hollywood. So, in some ways, Bee's cottage is the closest representation there is of Winslet's Rosehill Cottage and continues to be feted by fans of the film. Nancy Meyers, the director of the movie, even got in touch and told Bee that if she ever made a sequel, they would have to use her cottage.

It is not hard to understand the fuss. Bee's Cottage, which is called the Old Post Office, is a picture-perfect Cotswold cottage. It was built in the early sixteenth century from coursed Cotswold stone rubble and has a steeply pitched, thatched roof. The front of the house is like a child's drawing—two windows on the ground floor, two above, and a pleasingly off-centre front door between them, with a lavender-lined path leading up to it. If you were to try to imagine the archetype of an English country cottage, this would be it (as proven by the set designers of *The Holiday*). Bee believes it was originally built as two cottages, which explains the irregular positioning of the door.

The cottage lies within a small village in a river valley in North Oxfordshire. It was a local shop that first drew Bee to the village. She was searching for a place to rent in the area as she was about to move her youngest daughter to a school nearby. One day, passing a sign advertising the shop, she drove into the village in search of something for lunch and, as she got out of the car, spotted the Old Post Office. She was instantly smitten and then spied, almost hidden in the undergrowth, a For Sale sign. Bee knocked on the door and was met by a delightful couple, and as soon as she walked through "it felt like coming home." And so it was, because Bee was born in a cottage that looks rather like the Old Post Office, albeit in the somewhat grander surroundings of Windsor

OPPOSITE: Bee's cottage in the snow, channeling the cottage from *The Holiday*

A bench in the boot room gets a cushion by Osborn Interiors made in a grain sack material. The basket below was bought from Station Mill Antiques.

Great Park (next to the late Queen Elizabeth, the Queen Mother's house). Bee was born in a bedroom in Rose Cottage, was christened in the Royal Chapel, and has happy memories of growing up in that quaint and adorable house. So really it comes as no surprise to her that after living in ten different houses since first being married, Bee has finally ended up back in something so similar to her early childhood home.

Bee made an offer for the cottage on the spot. Her only caveat was that she needed to complete the purchase within three weeks so her daughter could start at her new school. She immediately moved in with daughter, husband, and four builders, and the seven of them slept under the same roof in the tiny house (the builders on the floor) as they started the renovations. The key to the architectural design was two small farm buildings at the back of the cottage. Bee was able to integrate these barns into the house to create a very large, multi-level living area. This permits residents and visitors to step beyond the original (and ancient) back wall into a modern sitting room, then down some steps into a contemporary kitchen, then back up again into an open-plan dining area—all contained within the same space. Bee has purposely retained its barn-like atmosphere. She repointed the original walls, keeping their original look—which includes bits of iron sticking out of the walls. The floors in the kitchen are oak planks with a colour wash on top, and the ceiling is made from a reclaimed floor that Bee found in a yard in Yorkshire.

The front door of the cottage opens straight into the sitting room, or "snug," which would have been the heart of the house. Its giant fireplace has an alcove for an oven and a "shepherd's seat," which Bee explains is where the original occupant of the house would have sat, quite literally next to the fire, in order to warm up after a day in the fields tending his animals. Next to this room is the study, which Bee calls "the Blue Room." Throughout the twentieth century this room housed the village's tiny post office, which is why the cottage is so named. Bee has designed and installed a large sofa bed in here for guests. Upstairs are three bedrooms, including Bee's spectacular oak-lined room and en suite bathroom.

The whole house is done in the style for which Bee is famous, which involves lots of natural materials alongside neutral, calming colour palettes. The cottage is both stylish and serene and is testament to Bee's clarity of vision. At Christmas she decorates the whole house in white and green, from presents, to tree, to table decorations. Bee admits, "If a present arrives from somewhere and doesn't match my palette, I will hide it. I am even tempted to re-wrap it. Isn't that awful?!" Absolutely not. After spending a day in this beautiful cottage, I want to be more like Bee.

In summer months, lavender lines the path up to the front door of the Old Post Office.

ABOVE: Bee designed the furniture for the Blue Room herself. This room is painted in Penny Black by Osborn Interiors.

RIGHT: The large fireplace in the Snug incorporates a "shepherd's seat."

ABOVE: The giant lampshade over the dining table was designed by Bee to match the off-centre apex of the room, and it was handmade in Malawi. It is 1.2 metres/3.9 feet across, and Bee almost couldn't get it into the house when it arrived.

Bee commissioned the "river" table and chose the oak for it.

RIGHT: A television cleverly disguised as a mirror in the kitchen's sitting area

OPPOSITE: The oak floors in the kitchen have a colour wash on top. The ceiling was originally a floor from another house that Bee found in a reclamation yard in Yorkshire. The pendant lights over the kitchen island are from PINCH.

ABOVE: All the furniture in the main bedroom was designed by Bee.

RIGHT: The spare bedroom is painted in Winter White—a hue mixed by Bee herself for Osborn Interiors. The same paint is used in the downstairs snug.

OPPOSITE: Bee's bathroom is centred around a magnificent free-standing tin slipper bath.

LEFT AND ABOVE: Bee created this space, affectionately dubbed the Love Shack, for her youngest daughter to hang out in with her friends.

The Columbarium

One of the many architectural delights of the Cotswolds is its plethora of ancient dovecotes.

These columbaria (to give them their Latin name—as it was the Romans who first introduced them to Britain) were built to house pigeons or doves. During the medieval period in Europe, the right to keep doves was the preserve of the aristocracy, and, as a result, many grand families built dovecotes in highly visible parts of their estates as status symbols. Often the dovecotes are all that remain of the original estates, as the main houses have been lost over the centuries. And such is the case with Hodges Barn, near Shipton Moyne. The original manor house to which it belonged, built by the Hodges family, burnt down in 1556, but what is left is breathtaking: a huge cruciform barn, which dates to 1499, on top of which sit a pair of square built dovecotes with Cotswold stone domed roofs (probably added later, towards the end of the seventeenth century). Hodges Barn continued to exist as an agricultural building until 1939, when it was converted into a highly original family home. Its architect, Lawrence Methuen, filled in the great entrances to the north and south of the building, through which carts were drawn, and instead installed formal sash windows and doors to create an elegant façade in the Queen Anne style.

Hodges barn is now home to Nicholas Hornby, his interior decorator wife, Amanda, and their three children. The house came into Nick's family in 1945, when it was bought by his great-grandmother Baroness Irene van Brienen. Irene had been brought up at Huys Clingendael, a notable seventeenth-century mansion house outside the Hague. Irene's portrait hangs in the main hall, and evidence of her Dutch origins remains throughout Hodges. Nick and Amanda have set about re-configuring the house for their needs, most notably building a discreet new wing to the east side. The architect Nick Hare helped Amanda plan the extension, and local architectural firm Verity and Beverley undertook the work. The new wing provides a spacious garden hall that doubles as a boot room (what Americans would call a mud room), and this is where the family and most visitors enter the house. A flower room sits off it, where Amanda arranges flowers from her cutting garden. "I'm obsessed by my dahlias and roses and tulips, and my peonies are fun too," says Amanda. "I'd rather buy my veg and grow flowers." Despite saying that, she also has a kitchen garden "with good asparagus beds and cavolo nero, aubergine, beetroot, and so on. But we don't

PREVIOUS PAGE: The twin cupolas of the original dovecote are visible above the Queen Anne–style façade of Hodges Barn.

OPPOSITE, TOP AND BOTTOM: The garden hall acts as the family's everyday entrance into the house and doubles as a boot room where they hang their hats and coats.

bother with potatoes, and we're lucky to have Highgrove farm shop [the Prince of Wales's house] just up the road." Nicholas is a keen gardener too, "although I'm more holistic, whereas Nick prefers spraying and chainsaws!" In June the gardens are open to the public, and tickets are always oversubscribed.

Amanda's office, looking out over a tree studded lawn, sits off one side of the hall, and on the opposite side is the door to the kitchen and the original part of the house. Underneath the garden hall is a vast basement, incorporating a billiards room, table tennis, a laundry room, and a cellar—a place of late-night fun particularly for the Hornby children.

The kitchen is a glorious space created from the several smaller rooms that existed in Nicholas's parents' day. Painted in pale blue and white, with a polished concrete floor and flooded with natural light from its dual aspect windows, it is a supremely calm room—perfect for absorbing the bustle of busy family life. Pops of colour are provided by pillar box red metal stools around the green marble topped island, and warmth comes from the fire "which is lit three hundred days a year" and surrounded by a Provençal chimneypiece.

The kitchen leads through to the main hall and a magnificent floating staircase that rises through the centre of the house. The drawing room, which is set up with two card tables, runs off it, as does a pretty dining room with a circular table and French windows leading out to the south lawn. Amanda's skills as an interior decorator are evident wherever one's gaze lands. "I love creating vistas, little still lives everywhere." It is an art she learnt at the start of her career when, after studying fashion and textiles at university, she found herself in Hong Kong, dressing the windows of the city's most prestigious department store. There she quickly discovered that styling the homeware section and creating sets "was far more interesting than dressing mannequins." Back in London she started helping friends decorate their houses, and her business grew organically from there. An early job was doing up a flat for Christiane Amanpour. "I think interiors should be timeless," says Amanda, "mixing old with new and layering for interest."

The first floor is home to the family bedrooms, and the floor above is dedicated to guests and includes the spectacular "four poster room" that sits underneath a domed ceiling in one of the columbaria. All the bedrooms are quite different, but all are beautifully wallpapered and full of fabulous fabrics that reflect Amanda's love of textiles. And at the top of the house, under the eaves, is a dormitory that can sleep up to seven children. "The girls used to come home from boarding school with a bevy of friends and sleep up there with them—in fact, they still do," says Amanda. Like the doves of five hundred years ago coming home to roost.

ABOVE: In the flower room, cupboards around the butler's sink are painted in Card Room Green by Farrow and Ball.

LEFT: The kitchen is created from the several smaller rooms that existed in Nicholas's parents' day, painted in pale blue and white, with a polished concrete floor, and flooded with natural light.

OPPOSITE AND ABOVE: The kitchen leads through to the main hall and a magnificent floating staircase that rises through the centre of the house.

RIGHT: The Hornbys have different-sized tops for the table, so they can seat up to sixteen in the dining room. The wallpaper is by Nicholas Herbert.

OPPOSITE: Amanda and Nicholas uncovered the dome in the four-poster bedroom. It had been a flat ceiling before. The bed is dressed in a Bennison fabric with a Jean Monro lining. The bed itself, with its painted candy-stripe pillars, was given to Nick's parents as a wedding present.

ABOVE LEFT: The *carnival de nis* tulips on the bedroom's chest of drawers are from Amanda's cutting garden.

ABOVE RIGHT: The marble over the bath in the four-poster bathroom is from the same quarry that provided for the Palace of Versailles. Amanda admits to being "obsessed by stone."

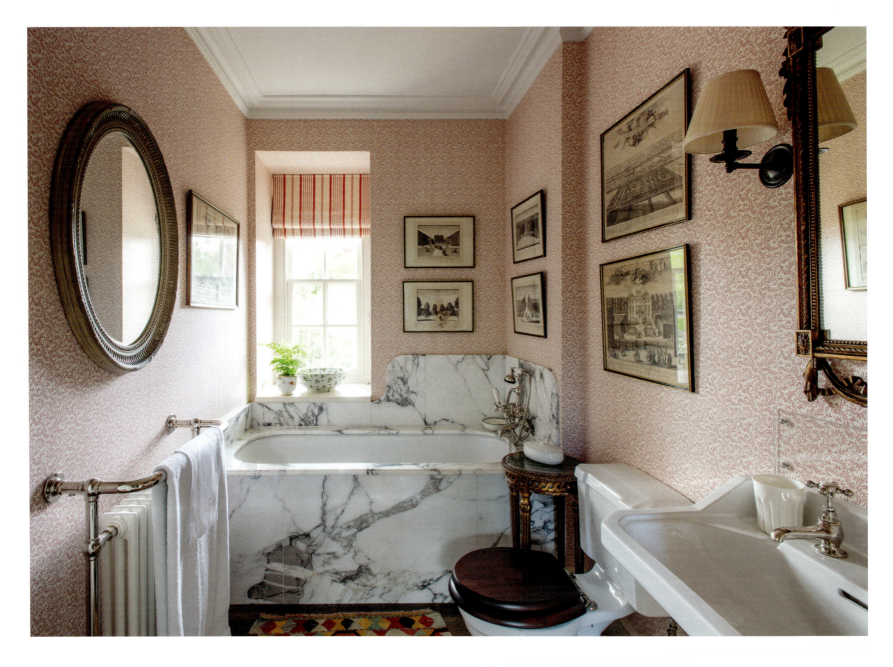

ABOVE: Decorated with antique prints of Clingendael—Irene's ancestral home—this bathroom adjoins the pomegranate bedroom.

OPPOSITE: The pomegranate bedroom is named after the *braquenié* wallpaper by Pierre Frey.

THE COLUMBARIUM | 59

OPPOSITE AND ABOVE LEFT: In the main bedroom, the portrait at the end of the bed is of Amanda's grandmother Elizabeth Wallop, by society photographer Dorothy Wilding. The etching above the bed is by the Australian artist Arthur Boyd and was given to the Hornbys as a wedding present.

ABOVE RIGHT: The studies of the children over the bath were done by Madeleine Rampling—a cousin of Nicholas.

ABOVE: The lamps in the hummingbird bedroom are converted vases that the Hornbys brought back from their time in Hong Kong. There are prints of Clingendael—Irene's ancestral home— in this room. The small, low gilt bench was bought from Christie's.

RIGHT: Featuring bunting left over from celebrations for the Queen's Jubilee, the top-floor dormitory also shows off vintage quilts bought in Tetbury and a collection of old toys, many from Amanda's own childhood. The wallpaper is by Manuel Canovas.

The Mason's House

The Cotswolds is built on a bedrock of fossil-rich, Jurassic oolitic limestone. This famous stone, from which the houses in this book are built, weathers to what is often described as a golden or honeyed hue. But, as J. B. Priestley wrote in his great travelogue *English Journey*, "the truth is that it has no colour that can be described. Even when the sun is obscured and the light is cold, these walls are still faintly warm and luminous, as if they knew the trick of keeping the lost sunlight of centuries glimmering about them."

The very finest of this stone historically came from the twin villages of Great Barrington and Little Barrington, which lie either side of the River Windrush, some three miles west of Burford. The stone mined and quarried here (since the fourteenth century) has helped create some of the finest buildings in the country: Christ Church College, Oxford; the Royal Chapel of St. George's, Windsor; Hampton Court Palace; the Sheldonian Theatre, Oxford; and Blenheim Palace, to name just a few. As a result, many successful masons have lived in the Barringtons over the centuries, the most famous being members of the Strong family.

Thomas Strong owned a quarry in Little Barrington in the latter half of the seventeenth century. He is renowned for being master mason to Sir Christopher Wren and actually laid the foundation stone for St. Paul's Cathedral with his own hands. On a somewhat smaller scale, Thomas built himself a home next to the site of his quarry in Little Barrington. Puffets, as it is called today (presumably because it later came to be owned by a family of that name), is a handsome ashlar terrace block of what originally would have been three cottages. With its mullioned windows and moulded architraves and stone door hoods on moulded brackets, all built from that gorgeous lustrous stone, it is a quintessential Cotswold building. Three and a half centuries on, it overlooks the sunken hollow of what once was a quarry and is now the village green, with the Tight brook running through it towards the River Windrush below. Its setting makes up what Pevsner described as "one of the most appealing village scenes in the Cotswolds." And it is now home to Lord and Lady Howard of Effingham and their twin children.

For Tatiana Howard, the Cotswolds is a long way from her birthplace in Peru. She is the youngest of thirteen, and each sibling was sent to Europe for

OPPOSITE: Puffets sits above the village green in Little Barrington.

an adventure after school. Tatiana arrived in London from Lima "a bit like Paddington bear," aged eighteen and barely speaking a word of English. She moved into a flat with one of her older sisters, but her sister soon hotfooted it to Italy with a boyfriend. Stuck for something to do, Tatiana signed up to a history-of-art course at Sotheby's. This, in turn, led to studying at the Inchbald School of Design and a passion for interior decoration. One by one, all of Tatiana's siblings returned to Peru, but she instead set up a successful design company called Tatiana Tafur (her maiden name) and has never left. It was still some years before she met Ed (son of the 7th Earl of Effingham), who introduced her to the delights of the English countryside. One day, whilst visiting friends in Oxfordshire, they drove through Burford—up the famously beautiful high street—and Tatiana just knew they had to come and live in the Cotswolds. After months of searching around Kingham and Northleach and all along the Windrush Valley, they eventually found Puffets. It was a weekend house at first, but as soon as the children were school age the Howards bought the cottage next door and created a permanent home.

It is said, though perhaps apocryphally, that Little Barrington is the most listed village in England, and it is certainly true that nearly every house here has an historic preservation order on it. Puffets is no exception, and so the Howards were extremely careful in their sympathetic approach to combining the cottages and building a kitchen extension to the back. What they have created is a heavenly home that utterly preserves the original nature of Thomas Strong's house. Traditional Cotswold cottages are often extremely picturesque from the outside but dark, low ceilinged, and somewhat cramped within. Not so with Puffets, which is surprisingly light and spacious. This is partly due to the Howards, who, for example, combined the sitting room of the original house with its hall to create a large, double-length drawing room with a fireplace at both ends. But it is also down to the generous proportions determined by Thomas Strong, who, when designing a house for himself, must have been influenced by the grander buildings he had been exposed to. Hence the mullioned windows that are of a far more lavish scale than is usual for a house of this size. The new kitchen has a vaulted, beamed green oak ceiling. Tatiana decided that, as it was to double as their dining room, it should have as formal a feel as possible. And the Howards love to entertain in here.

Throughout the house are examples of Tatiana Tafur furniture, along with textured wall coverings that are made from a sustainable material called abaca—sister to the banana plant. The first floor of the house has three bedrooms and Tatiana's study. The floor above is where each of the children has a bedroom and a bathroom and enough space to have their friends stay.

A highlight of every year is Giffords Circus taking up residence in the meadows next to the village for ten days or so in the summer. This much beloved, old-fashioned outfit has attained cult status in the Cotswolds, and the Howards, like many of the villagers, go night after night to listen to the raucous band and watch the prancing ponies, the extraordinary acrobats, and Tweedy the Clown. To get there they walk across the village green and past the honeyed stone houses and cross the river at Strong's Causeway, built by the great man Thomas himself, to connect the two Barrington villages into one happy community.

ABOVE: Purple "lollipop" alliums in the back garden of the house

OVERLEAF: The spice boxes to the side of the fireplace date back to the 1600s. "The historic listing people were more excited by these than anything else," says Tatiana.

The curtains are made of fabric by Bennison.

OPPOSITE AND ABOVE: "My vision was based on the Nicholas Haslam fabric on the back of the chairs and the curtains. I designed the rest of the kitchen to match." The console is from Charles Pollock. Over the kitchen table is a Niermann Weeks hanging light.

LEFT: The desk in the study is a 1940s design by Lucien Rolland. The painting is by an artist named Alain Switzer, a present from a friend. The pre-Columbian weave fabric on the wall is more than two thousand years old.

The sconce lights on the hallway wall are by Tatiana Tarfur, as is the "Barrington" wallcovering (named after the village).

ABOVE LEFT: The top floor of the house, which Tatiana calls the nursery floor, is a dedicated space for her children.

ABOVE RIGHT: The painted headboard in this child's room is from Tatiana Tarfur. The walls are painted in Plaster by Farrow and Ball. The curtain material is by Bennison.

ABOVE LEFT: The staircase outside the master bedroom, with its bannister rope

ABOVE RIGHT AND OPPOSITE TOP: The main bedroom's Venetian-style bed and dressing table and stool were all hand painted in Italy to Tatiana's own designs. Nicholas Herbert material is on the headboard. Portraits of the twins are by the niece of a friend.

RIGHT: Tatiana designed the bathroom cupboards (although she admits to being heavily inspired by Jane Churchill). A local joiner made them up with abaca wallcovering behind. Elephant Breath Farrow and Ball paint is on the walls. The pink stool is designed by Tatiana and called "Puffets." It is covered in a Nicholas Herbert fabric.

The Old Rectory

If the Cotswolds is for many Britons their ideal landscape, then an Old Rectory is their ideal house. No type of building in England is more evocative, celebrated, or lusted over, and I doubt there is a more resonant term in the lexicon of English architecture. Old Rectories conjure up images of croquet on the lawn, sash windows, cucumber sandwiches, church bells, fetes, and country parsons snoozing away the afternoon in their libraries. The homesick war poet Rupert Brooke summons the romantic idyll of the rectory in his famous poem "The Old Vicarage, Grantchester." He ends the ode with a wistful prayer that life there remains unchanged: "Yet stands the church clock at ten to three? And is there honey still for tea?" And this is not the rectory's only literary association. You will find it in the pages of George Eliot and Anthony Trollope. Lewis Carroll and the Brontë sisters grew up in rectories. As did Jane Austen, whose heroine in *Northanger Abbey* dreamt of "the unpretending comfort of a well-connected parsonage." George Bernard Shaw chose to live in one, and so did Sir John Betjeman. (And not just any rectory. The Old Rectory, Farnborough, which the poet laureate bought in the 1940s, was once voted by *Country Life* magazine as the most beautiful Old Rectory in England.) Charles Moore, the former editor of the *Telegraph*, has set up a society celebrating Old Rectories (whose patron is Sir Tom Stoppard). And there have been several books written about them, including one by Deborah Alun-Jones in which she describes "the archetypal Georgian rectory, nestling by the ancient church it was built to serve" as being "the embodiment of the English rural idyll."

So, what are these houses and why do they inspire such great affection? Old Rectories are former church houses built by or for Anglican priests near to the churches for which they were responsible for. Rectory building on a large scale began during Queen Anne's reign and continued apace during the Georgian and Victorian eras. And it is Georgian rectories with their generous proportions, large windows, and classical lines that remain the most cherished and sought after today.

They are in many ways the perfect house. They are invariably handsome buildings and spacious without being too large. They have a prime location within a village. Because of the cultured nature of their original inhabitants, they often have fine libraries and carefully sculpted, well-stocked gardens. And

OPPOSITE: The perfectly symmetrical façade of the Old Rectory, built in 1788.

OPPOSITE TOP: York paving stones and a water feature on the terrace, designed by Lesley and inspired by a terrace she had seen in Jaipur. "I love the sound of water in the garden."

OPPOSITE BOTTOM: There was an existing pool, but Lesley re-surfaced it, decked it, and built a pool house. The pool is open all year round and is more like a water feature in winter.

An evergreen bamboo behind the pool is a great screen and creates a slightly tropical atmosphere.

of course, their nearest neighbour is invariably a church, which in the Cotswolds means a richly appointed piece of ecclesiastical architecture.

Lesley Cooke's Old Rectory, featured here, is a perfect archetype. Built in 1788 along classic Georgian lines, it has two storeys of five windows with simple architraves and keystones, and a parapet below its hipped roof. It sits on the edge of its village with pretty gardens and far-reaching views over the countryside beyond. The diocese sold the house in the 1950s, and Lesley bought it in 2010 and began its restoration.

Major structural repairs to the roof were required, along with extensive internal refurbishments. The existing coach house and stables were converted into a block with ancillary accommodation, an office, and a cinema room. A kitchen extension was built to replace a dilapidated flat built in the 1960s to connect the main house to the stables. The grounds were landscaped and a new pool house created.

Lesley was determined to have a large, well-equipped kitchen. The new extension contains two large islands, a pair of double-doored fridges, and both an oven and an AGA (that iconic cast-iron cooker so beloved of English country house owners). Lesley didn't want the look of a modern fitted kitchen and instead has opted for open shelving and has filled the room with antique furniture. With its open fire, ceiling lantern, and triple aspect, it is simultaneously light-filled and cosy. Lesley designed a butler's pantry to connect the kitchen to the house, with a concealed jib door leading into the dining room. The pantry's four dishwashers and array of glasses betray the Cookes' love of entertaining. Dinner parties are always candlelit, and the absence of electric light in the dining room gives guests a sense of how life would have been in the eighteenth century.

Lesley, who is an interior decorator and landscape designer, was keen to embrace the history of the house and furnish it in a style that complements the original interior. Hence, for example, her four-poster bed was chosen because it fills the volume of a big Georgian bedroom, and her black marbled, 1920s-style bathroom reflects the era when houses like this would have first adopted modern plumbing and introduced new bathrooms.

Lesley's study on the ground floor occupies what would have been the parish room—an office where the rector would have conducted local church business. A clergyman in the nineteenth century created a doorway into this room from the garden, so he could receive his parishioners without them disturbing his family. How those parishioners must have sighed with pleasure, as I do today, as they made their way through the rectory gardens to this most serene and quintessentially English of houses.

ABOVE AND RIGHT: Around the kitchen table is a selection of chairs that come from three sets of six chairs that are mixed up around the house and in bedrooms. Lesley sourced the farmhouse table from Tetbury, which is something of a mecca for antiques in the Cotswolds.

OPPOSITE: The dining room is decorated with De Gournay wallpaper. The French chandelier above the table is one of a pair (its twin is in the drawing room). It is not wired and is only used with real candles. A jib door leading into the butler's pantry and the kitchen beyond disappears into the wall.

ABOVE: Lesley's study, in what was once the "parish room"

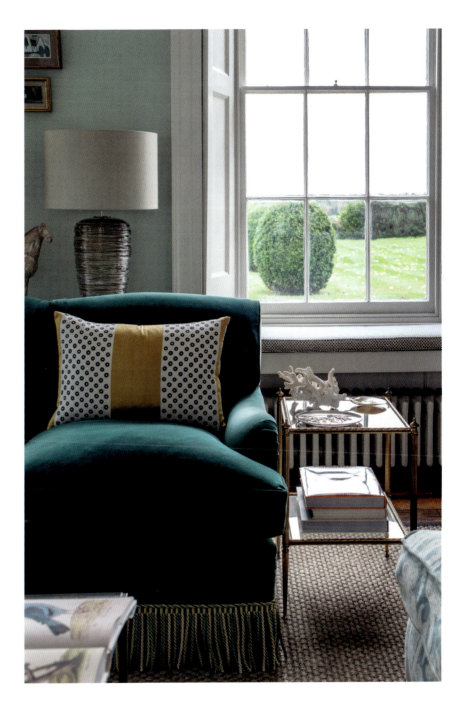

LEFT AND ABOVE: Huge mirrors on either side of the drawing room fireplace were sourced in the Kings Road in London. The room is painted in Sung Grey by Papers and Paints (one of Patrick Baty's historical ranges). The painting over the fireplace is by a British landscape artist whose work drifts into abstraction. The Cooks use the drawing room all the time. "I often light a fire in the afternoons, and my husband lights a cigar," says Lesley.

Lesley remodeled a bedroom to create a big dressing room and bathroom. The bathroom embraces a 1920s style, in keeping with when modern bathrooms were first being put into houses like this.

OPPOSITE AND ABOVE: The four-poster bed in the main bedroom helps fills the volume of a large, traditional Georgian room. The wallpaper is by De Gournay.

ABOVE: Lesley liked the garret feel of this room, now her daughter's bedroom, which she covered in pink toile wallpaper by Manuel Canovas.

RIGHT: This bedroom under the eaves in the old coach house used to be a hayloft.

ABOVE LEFT: The oversized bedhead in the Blue Room was designed by Lesley, to complement the high ceilings in this guest bedroom.

ABOVE RIGHT: Bowood paper by Colefax and Fowler accents a second guestroom. Lesley likes to put something black in every room she decorates.

The "Hovel"

One of the charming things about Cotswold houses is that they are, more often than not, roofed in the same mellow stone as their walls. Muffities is a typical example, and its unusual name denotes a particular size of Cotswold stone tile, examples of which you can see cloaking the cottage's roof, alongside equally wonderfully named *wivetts*, *tants*, and *cussomes*.

The owner of Muffities affectionately refers to the cottage as a "hovel," because that effectively is what it once was: an extremely humble dwelling for a farm worker, originally with just one room downstairs and one above. But the irony is obvious as soon as you step inside this exquisitely decorated, book- and flower-filled house. It is a haven of culture and beauty that shows off its owner's passion for collecting art and furniture.

Muffities is home to James Mackie, former senior director of Sotheby's, and his partner, the writer and gardener Arthur Parkinson. A hovel it isn't, but it certainly is small in size. James bought it in 2016 and then spent three years meticulously planning its refurbishment. As he explains, "A project like this is an exercise in winning every extra square inch that you can. We all love the idea of a little English cottage, but you have to work at them quite hard and make every corner earn its keep if they're to make sense for modern living."

One enters through a porch straight into the sitting room and the heart of the house. An inglenook fireplace, with a recessed space for a bread oven, is integrated with the original stone staircase that winds its way behind the chimneypiece up into the bedroom above. It is a peculiar piece of architectural design unique to the Cotswolds, and one that died out around 1700 and therefore dates the cottage to sometime before that. It is a challenging room, as, along with the front door, there are four other doors leading off it. But despite this James has managed to turn it into a warm and cosy space where he and Arthur sit in the evenings and in winter. There is no television in the house, but a cinema screen pulls down from the ceiling of the sitting room and a projector hidden in the wall allows them to watch films. James loves to play with texture. There is seagrass on the floor and North African and Middle Eastern textiles on the sofa, but also old gilt, mahogany, silver-mercury, lacquer, and oak. Not to mention feather, in the form of a stuffed barn owl in one corner of the room. The important thing, says James, is "a stimulating mix to stop things looking staid. Rooms would be so plain and boring without it."

OPPOSITE: Muffities is named after its Cotswold stone roof tiles.

The garden sunshade is from Cutter Brooks in Stow-on-the-Wold.

The sitting room leads through an open doorway into the Book Room. This is a completely new extension but one that James designed to look as though it might have been added in the mid-nineteenth century, with a deeply recessed Victorian-style bay window. And then, continuing the narrative, James panelled the room in an Arts and Crafts style that looks as if it might have been put in a century or so ago. James drew the panels himself onto the freshly plastered walls, and then a local joiner built them to his design. The panels are various different sizes to fit around the room, "but all within a range so as not to be discordant," and some with cleverly designed roundels to fit the wall sconces. James, after a lifetime of collecting books, had long dreamt of a library, and the bookshelves in the room are designed to house his large tomes that focus on Impressionist art, Georgian furniture, interior decoration, and the English country house. But the bookcase was also designed to support a wonderful classical pediment, "a piece of architectural salvage in the style of William Kent—whom I am an enormous acolyte of."

The room is painted in Mummy by Edward Bulmer, which James points out is not as sweet as it sounds but is named so because it is the colour of mummified remains. "But I love Mummy, because it is the most marvellous activator for all the other elements—a foil for the books and the furniture. It's got great character but doesn't shout at you." A deep interest in, and passion for, colour is something that James and Arthur share. And as we step from the Book Room into the garden, the blast of purples and pinks that greets us is invigorating. The main bed is filled with foxgloves and a profusion of roses with wonderful names like Gertrude Jekyll, Desdemona, and Sceptred Isle. Pretty pots of crimson Lord Bute and Turkish Coffee pelargoniums sit on a stone-top table. There is no doubting the hand of Arthur, who alongside being head florist to garden supremo Sarah Raven is also the author of two books, *The Pottery Gardener* and *The Flower Yard*.

It was a mutual love of flowers that brought James and Arthur together. The pair met at the Chelsea Flower Show, when James was so taken by the flowers on Arthur's stand that he stopped to ask for a crib sheet of the varietal names. They have been together ever since.

They quickly discovered another mutual passion—that of rural Derbyshire and specifically Chatsworth House—possibly England's finest country house. Arthur grew up not far from there and as a child wrote to Debo, the late Duchess of Devonshire, which started a long correspondence. James, meanwhile, spent many holidays on a family farm nearby and, when studying architectural history at Sheffield University, wrote part of his dissertation on the house. Later, when he joined Sotheby's, he spent time at Chatsworth, as the 12th Duke was

deputy chairman of the auction house. Throughout Muffities are various early prints of the house. There are also many pieces of art that reflect James's career. After a period at Bonhams, James ran the Print Department at Sotheby's and, later, became head of Impressionist and Modern Art. Art remains a passion. He recalls a standout moment during the sale of a version of Edvard Munch's *The Scream*: "I arrived in New York jet lagged and went to the office first thing in the morning. The porters unscrewed the packing case and left me alone with the picture. The colours were so vibrant I had an actual physical reaction to it." Now retired from the hectic world of the auction rooms, James has started an art advisory and interior decoration business.

We head into the kitchen for tea, and James describes how the room would have originally been a stable for animals. Waiting for us is a supremely decadent, cream-filled Victoria sponge made by Arthur. It's so pretty that Mark insists on photographing it. James quickly moves to sweep up some crumbs dropped from the cake: "I don't want your readers thinking I live in an actual hovel!" There's little chance of that.

The bureau in the Book Room is from Max Rollit. It has a wonderfully untouched surface. "I hate things that are over polished," says James. "It's so stultifying.'" The eighteenth-century chairs on either side have a chinoiserie decoration that was probably added in the early twentieth century.

LEFT: In the Book Room, the chinoiserie-lacquered long case clock is English from the 1730s, a present from James's parents for his fortieth birthday.

ABOVE: The armchair in the window is an incredibly comfortable original from Howard and Sons—the Victorian company that started making revolutionary feather and down sofas in an era of horsehair. The chairs are now cult objects. This one is covered in Rockbird by GP & J Baker.

ABOVE AND RIGHT: The bedcover is an antique locally made quilt. The curtain fabric is Strawberry Leaf by John Fowler. The metallic Brownrigg lampshades are a way of introducing fun and a bit of the unexpected. All the pictures in the bedroom have a resonance to James and Arthur, particularly the little chalk and pencil drawing of Chatsworth. The trim along the top of the walls is by Lewis and Wood.

ABOVE LEFT AND RIGHT: This bedroom is not named for its William Morris Willow Bough wallpaper, but after a great friend, whose surname is Morris, who stays there often. James designed the bookshelves and a bed board on the angled back wall, which originally would have been the outside of the cottage. A stuffed puffin sits on a 1920s chinoiserie bracket above the bed. The deep colour of the woodwork is another paint developed by Farrow and Ball in collaboration with the Natural History Museum. A pine chest of drawers is painted to look like burr walnut.

ABOVE: James's bathroom

RIGHT: The sitting room is the least altered room in the house; James painted the beams to make the room look less heavy and took out a mantel shelf with gargoyles. He hung a George II mirror with candelabra above the fire. The plaster fleurs-de-lis are a curiosity. James can't imagine that they are later than twentieth-century but wonders who set them in.

ABOVE: James has converted a tiny corner of the corridor leading to the downstairs loo into a bar. What was nothing is now a place of joy and fun, painted in Farrow and Ball's Arsenic and decorated with hanging early nineteenth-century Spode plates.

LEFT: Like the rest of the house, the kitchen is an exercise in making a small space work as hard as possible. The Arts and Crafts oak table comfortably seats six (the perfect number for a supper party) but can seat a couple more. The taps are from deVOL. A wonderful hare print sits in its original 1780s frame behind the original glass. The chairs around the kitchen table are from a dealer called Simon Myers in Yorkshire.

The High House

High House is exactly that. It sits on high, dominating the centre of the tiny village of Winstone, which itself is sited on top of a high plateau overlooking the Frome Valley. It is a perfect Georgian dolls' house whose appealing symmetry extends from its twin chimneypieces down to the matching bay trees standing sentry on either side of its entrance. The front garden is filled with tulips when we visit. White clematis grows up its flanking stone walls, and a lavender-lined path leads up to the front of the house, which is adorned with wisteria. Entering under the hipped porch (which was a nineteenth-century addition), one finds that the interior of the house is equally as pleasing. Everything is just so, from the fetching wallpapers of the bedrooms right down to a gently snoring cockerpoo, named Pudding, lying in an elegant wicker basket in the hall.

High House is home to Caroline Baker and her teenage daughter, Tatiana. They yearned for the countryside but needed to be a commutable distance from London, and so the Cotswolds made perfect sense. It was the first house they came to see, and it was love at first sight for both of them. "As soon as we came round the corner and saw the house with the view beyond, that was it. It was a blissful early summer day, and the owners had left the doors and windows open. The house exuded happiness." Caroline bought it on the spot and then set about creating a peaceful haven as a counterfoil to her extremely busy working life in London.

Caroline owns and runs an eponymous company that specialises in property management for some of the highest-net-worth families in the world. So it comes as no surprise that her own home in the Cotswolds is immaculate and bustling with helpers. It is also supremely feminine in nature, but not fussy. Caroline decorated much of it herself but also recruited the help of some of her Cotswold-based interior designer friends. Leonora Birts, for instance, helped her choose the pretty pink Cuisse de Nymph colour by Edward Bulmer for the hall, and Rosanna Bossom has recently re-done Caroline's bedroom and bathroom. On the ground floor there are three reception rooms and a kitchen leading off the generous hallway; a smart dining room, an elegant drawing

OPPOSITE: The perfect doll's house symmetry of High House

ABOVE AND OPPOSITE: French prints, from a gallery on the New Kings Road in London, range along the hall. Pudding, the cockerpoo, sleeps in a wicker OKA bed underneath a fabulous collection of straw hats. "I love hats," says Caroline; "I get them from Locks, and I live in a trilby in London during the winter." The sofa is covered in a fabric by Soane.

room, along with a cosy sitting room full of photographs, just the place to curl up in the evenings. There are four bedrooms, with accompanying bathrooms, spread over the two floors above. To create extra space, Caroline has built a large light-filled office a few metres beyond the back of the house. But it's not just a place of work; it also contains an upright Steinway piano where Caroline likes to practice for an hour every day.

Alongside her office is quite easily the smartest shepherd's hut in the Cotswolds. These portable cabins have a history stretching back hundreds of years but reached peak popularity during the nineteenth century, when they were given corrugated iron roofs and cast-iron wheels. They were built as one-room shelters for shepherds and wheeled to remote corners of estates so that farmers could be closer to their sheep during lambing season. These huts, or wagons, would typically contain a small stove for heating and a raised bed with room for orphaned lambs underneath. Of course, with the advent of modern farming practices, large covered barns, and four-wheel-drive vehicles, the practice died out, but shepherds' huts remain immensely popular for glamping. Victorian shepherds would be astounded by Caroline's version, which is traditional-looking on the outside but, on the inside, contains a lavishly upholstered four-poster bed and a gleaming, freestanding copper bath.

One of the joys of living in Winstone is its proximity to the glorious market town of Cirencester, just five miles to the south. Founded by the ancient Romans in the first century AD, Corinium Dobunnorum, as it was then known, was the second biggest city in Roman Britain (after Londinium). At its peak it was home to more than ten thousand residents and boasted a vast amphitheatre whose massive earthwork remains can still be seen on the outskirts of the town. There is little else in the way of Roman architecture evident today, but the town's importance to the area continues. In fact, Cirencester is often referred to as the Capital of the Cotswolds. It is a bustling town whose market square is dominated by a beautiful fifteenth-century parish church (one of the largest in Britain) built from honeycomb-yellow Cotswold stone. Caroline is particularly fond of Black Jack Street, which sits in the shadow of the church. The street's name is said to derive from a soot-blackened statue of St. John the Baptist that once stood on the church's tower. Here you can find one of the oldest butchers in Britain and also a famously fabulous children's bookshop named after its owner, Octavia. The town is also home to a theatre, a polo club (often hosting sporting members of the royal family), and the Royal Agricultural University, founded in 1842, whose alumni run many of the Cotswolds' finest estates. It is both the spiritual and geographical heart of the Cotswolds. Not a bad place to have on one's doorstep.

ABOVE: The wallpaper in the downstairs loo is Pineapple by Soane. The chickens were a present from a friend.

LEFT: Above the fireplace in the cosy sitting room are ink drawings of flora. Caroline bought them from King's Court Galleries on the Fulham Road in London.

ABOVE: In the dining room there is a portrait of Pudding "by my great girlfriend Carrots." The Lewis and Wood wallpaper is a Cotswold scene based on a village near Tetbury.

OPPOSITE: The kitchen contains a very à la mode white AGA.

ABOVE AND OPPOSITE, TOP LEFT: The Cotswolds-based interior designer Rosie Bossom recently redecorated Caroline's bedroom.

OPPOSITE, TOP RIGHT: Caroline's prettily decorated en suite bathroom with its free-standing pink bath.

OPPOSITE, BOTTOM: Tatiana's bedroom has a "half tester" bed with a canopy projecting from the wall.

OPPOSITE: Inside the shepherd's hut. Hidden behind the screen at the back of the bed is a free-standing copper bath.

ABOVE: Caroline's desk sits in front of a bookcase which is adorned with blue and white china pots—a motif that is repeated throughout the house.

The Farm Worker's Cottage

*J*ust to be clear, Alexandra Tolstoy is not a farm worker. But she does live in an eighteenth-century farm worker's cottage in a tiny hamlet surrounded by some of the loveliest farmland in Oxfordshire. And the Anglo-Russian countess has just been watching a new television series about farming life in the Cotswolds with her three children: "We are all totally gripped by it and now desperate to become farmers." I'm not quite sure, though, where she would find the time, as she already juggles running an antiques and textiles business (the Tolstoy Edit) alongside organising riding adventures in Kyrgyzstan, journalism, and being a single mother.

One of life's natural adventurers, Alexandra has explored some of the wildest parts of the world, not least becoming the first person since Marco Polo's time to travel the five thousand miles of the Silk Road on horse and camel. So the gentle hills of rural Oxfordshire must seem very dull. "But this is where I grew up," says Alexandra. "My parents are only a few miles away, and this tiny cottage is our haven." It is certainly cosy. The front door opens into the kitchen, whose low-slung ceiling presents dangerous beams to the even moderately tall. Alexandra laughs as she tells me that she bought the house from a jockey friend (the Grand National winner Marcus Armytage) whose small frame was perfectly suited to it.

There is a pleasingly old-fashioned air to the cottage. When Alexandra bought it in 2004, she was determined to give it a traditional look that reflected its origins. This included hiring a specialist plasterer who used time-honoured methods to lime plaster the walls and ceilings, just as they would have been when the cottage was first built. This gives them a wonderful, slightly uneven depth and a texture that takes on a colour of its own as it ages. Alexandra touches it up with a white limewash every so often. She removed the wooden windowsills and skirting boards and plastered them as well. Continuing with the traditional theme, she painted the woodwork in the house a rich, dark brown (Wainscot from Farrow and Ball's archive collection). There are Bakelite light switches on the wall and even an old Bakelite telephone next to her bed. There are almost no concessions to modernity, and crossing the threshold feels like stepping into a previous century. It is Alexandra's view that "an old house like this should have a connection to history and its roots."

OPPOSITE: A garden path, fringed with summer blooms, leads to the front door of the cottage.

The kitchen is very much the heart of the house: The children love to bake, and Alexandra loves to entertain. Often, during the winter months, this room is lit only by candles, which makes it incredibly atmospheric. In the summer, the family sets a table onto the lawn in front of the cottage and dines outdoors.

In terms of decoration, over the years Alexandra has gradually filled the cottage with a collection of antique English furniture, porcelain, and vintage fabrics, to create a little slice of old rural England. But there are also touches that reflect her Russian heritage. There is a Russian valance around the bed, for example, and a small oil painting of Cossack horsemen in one corner of the sitting room, and there are religious icons in most rooms.

Alexandra's grandfather fled from Russia as a small boy in 1920. He escaped the Bolsheviks and was smuggled out of the country by his English governess, who used a forged birth certificate to claim him as her own. Alexandra's father, Count Nikolai Tolstoy, was brought up as an Englishman, but he returns to Russia every so often to preside over a congregation of Tolstoys at Yasnaya Polyana—Leo Tolstoy's historic estate south of Moscow. Alexandra didn't feel particularly drawn to her Russian heritage until she travelled to Moscow as a young woman. She now travels back to Moscow frequently and has made sure that her children speak the language.

The children's bedroom looks a bit like something out of Goldilocks, with three beds of different sizes. It is a tiny space; however, the children love being there all together, and "the lack of indoor space forces them to be outside as much as possible."

The main bedroom, across the landing, is more spacious and grander in style. It is wallpapered and full of fabulous fabrics, from its orange velvet curtains to its Persian rug and the vintage quilt on the iron bedstead. The family all share a bathroom, which has tongue-and-groove panelling and is prettily decorated with nineteenth-century "sailors' valentines"—elaborate heart designs fashioned from shellwork. Alexandra is so enamoured by these pieces of antique shell craft that she commissioned the artist Sarah-Jane Axelby to re-create them in mixed media, which she sells as limited-edition prints in her online store.

Alexandra has a collector's passion, and the cottage is teeming with all manner of fascinating *objets*. "A lot of people think that living in a tiny cottage filled with antiques is totally impractical, but actually it is great," she says.

Unusually, especially as the cottage is miles from the nearest shop, Alexandra doesn't drive. "I never have. I spent my twenties on horseback, and driving in Moscow is far too dangerous." So she and the children take trains everywhere. "And walking is key to our lives. We walk everywhere. And when we come to

the cottage, we're completely stuck here, which is great for the imagination." As a result, the children know every inch of the land around the cottage. They fish in the river, play in the woods, bicycle along the Thames path, and ride at a nearby pony club. But recently the family have finally decided that they might like a car after all. And so Alexandra has begun taking driving lessons. Together they have chosen their ideal future vehicle—a predictably vintage Land Rover Defender. "I think it will probably change our lives," says Alexandra.

A vintage AGA oven sits in the very centre of the cottage.

LEFT AND ABOVE: A collection of local Bell pottery mugs sits near the butler's sink, whose backsplash is created from antique Delft tiles found in a shop on London's Portobello Road.

The wooden carvings above the kitchen counter come from Jubilee Hall in nearby Lechlade.

The farmhouse kitchen table came from Alexandra's aunt's old shop in Devizes, Crowman Antiques.

PREVIOUS SPREAD, ABOVE, AND OPPOSITE: The sitting room with its large open fire. The lime render above the fireplace has turned a pleasing yellow over time. The curtains are by Robert Kime. The military jacket came from Crowman Antiques. On the dresser are some of Alexandra's collection of Staffordshire figures, many of a Scottish theme.

ABOVE: In the main bedroom, the orange velvet curtains come from an antiques shop in Bath.

A Victorian cast-iron bed gets a splash of color from an American patchwork quilt.

Alexandra found the embroidered pheasants in a shop on Kensington Church Street in London.

One of the Russian touches in the cottage is the valance on Alexandra's bed, which is from Nathalie Farman-Farma at Decors Barbares.

RIGHT: Maria's old Welsh patchwork comes from the Tolstoy Edit, as do the vintage English eiderdowns on the children's beds.

ABOVE: The office is headquarters, where Alexandra plans her riding trips across central Asia. The stuffed goose "was a pet" and comes from Lechlade. She is building up a collection of books to replace the library she used to have in Moscow.

LEFT: The cloakroom. Alexandra embroidered her initials onto the towel hanging above the butler's sink.

The Arts and Crafts House

Clinging to the side of a hill high above the villages of Broadway, Buckland, and Laverton is the ancient stone-built hamlet of Snowshill. From its perch on top of the Cotswolds escarpment, it commands extraordinary views over an exquisite landscape below. Its height gives it its name, as, come winter, the snow settles here before anywhere else in the surrounding countryside. It is home to a handsome National Trust manor house, famed for its Arts and Crafts garden, and it is also the location of a house owned by Robin Smith Sulgar that is itself an exemplar of the Arts and Crafts style.

The Cotswolds is synonymous with the Arts and Crafts movement. This design philosophy, which flourished in England in the decades straddling the turn of the twentieth century, advocated traditional craftsmanship that married practicality with artistry, often drawing on medieval and folk styles of decoration. Many of its leading practitioners settled in the area during this period. They were following in the footsteps of the design giant William Morris, whose manor house in Kelmscott remains a place of pilgrimage for afficionados to this day. They were also drawn by the charm of its landscape, its rich craft tradition, and its unique existing architecture.

One of the architect designers who left their mark on the region was Charles Edward Bateman. Bateman was a Birmingham-based architect who rejected the highly ornate, gothic style of many of his Victorian peers as he turned his attention towards the Cotswolds. In 1916 he was commissioned to restore four ancient cottages in charming Snowshill. He completely remodelled the existing seventeenth-century buildings to create a large family home with a picturesque exterior and a practical arrangement of rooms inside. It is a masterpiece of Arts and Crafts restorative architectural design.

The Cotswolds stone house is an unusual L shape with a half-timbered link, with plasterwork, connecting the elevations. There are attractive mullion windows, fine stone dressings, and both hipped and gabled dormers. Inside we find great open fireplaces and flagstoned floors that date back centuries, alongside the wooden fittings and exposed stonework of Bateman's work.

The house was bought by Robin and her husband, Justin, a few years ago. The couple are both American—Robin originally from South Carolina and Justin from New York—but they met in London, where they were both working.

OPPOSITE: The front door leads into the oldest part of the house.

The flagstoned front hall

Their daughters were born in the UK, and the family divides its time between the Cotswolds and London.

Robin always had a love for interior design: After she renovated her own homes (including a previous house in the Cotswolds), friends started asking her for help with theirs. She now runs her own design studio and considers it a great privilege. "Working with people on their houses is incredibly intimate." Robin has a sympathetic approach to her renovations and design work: "It's important to be historically informed and respectful. This doesn't mean that everything needs to be period, but you should never fight the architecture of the house."

Her own house is pleasingly uncluttered, but not stark. "I always try to create soft, serene spaces but still with a bit of soul to them—I love a collected aesthetic—when a room feels like it has come together over time." She believes in preserving or enhancing historic architectural details as much as possible and admits to often being "worryingly obsessed with lighting," partial to low wattages, dimmers, and candlelight.

One enters the house into a tall-ceilinged reception hall, where a Spanish metal chandelier hangs over a large French mirrored-top table from the 1960s. The main staircase hall is adjacent, and steps down lead to a pair of beautifully timbered interconnecting reception rooms. When it comes to furniture, Robin has fairly eclectic tastes and a passion for sourcing antiques and vintage pieces. Geographically, she is all-embracing. In the drawing room, for example, there are Italian wall lights and Spanish leather-topped stools from the nineteenth century alongside eighteenth-century French armchairs and a Dutch bleached oak table. A carved wooden tribal stool came from Cameroon, and a little English bobbin table sits in the corner.

Follow the stairs back up and you reach the bright main bedroom wing, which boasts seven original leaded windows and half-timbered walls. The adjoining, longer wing containing three further bedrooms sits above the large dining room with the kitchen beyond.

French doors in the dining room lead out to the kitchen terrace, which looks out over the house's twenty acres of terraced gardens, woods, and ancient pastures leading down to a small lake. Robin admits, "It was the view that sold me the house." And what a view it is. It is quite literally breathtaking. I challenge anyone to step out onto the terrace and look up without having a sudden, small intake of breath. It is a quintessential Cotswolds landscape that is endlessly absorbing. It explains why Bronze Age settlers chose to inhabit this stunning spot thousands of years ago (and left behind a burial mound whose treasures can now be found in the British Museum). They must have been jolly cold come wintertime in their short woollen tunics, but it would have been worth it for such a view.

LEFT: The southern elevation of the house, which overlooks the lake below.

OVERLEAF: The zinc pendant lights hanging over the kitchen table are from the French House. Robin found the antique Italian refectory table at Lorfords Antiques in Tetbury. The walls are painted in Inferior Grey by Edward Bulmer.

The dining chairs are a mix of vintage pieces and Tolix-inspired copper and wood chairs. The ceiling is painted with Little Green's Roman Plaster.

OPPOSITE TOP AND BOTTOM, AND RIGHT: The drawing room is painted in Edward Bulmer Lilac Pink, which turns into a warm pink in the evening light.

The sofa is covered in jute, which Robin concedes is a bit impractical, but she loves the natural texture.

Furnishings include a pair of eighteenth-century French Bergères in yellow linen, antique studded leather stools from Spain, and an eighteenth-century French ebonized chest of drawers.

At right is a Scottish console with a pair of Vaughan table lamps sitting above. The handmade mahogany milking stool was a wedding gift.

ABOVE: Little Greene Loft White brightens the walls and floors; the side tables are hand painted.

LEFT: The upstairs landing. The bare walls draw the eye towards the extraordinary beams.

OPPOSITE TOP: Four coats of Little Green Loft White cover the floorboards: "I really like bedrooms in the countryside to feel light and fresh," says Robin.

The light fixture is a vintage metal chandelier; the oak chest of drawers is French and from the nineteenth century.

OPPOSITE BOTTOM: A pair of antique French beds that are, uniquely, not the same size. The floorboards are painted Little Greene Mid-G, a favourite colour that reminds Robin of the blue-grey porch floors of her childhood home.

A quintessential Cotswold view from the kitchen terrace

THE ARTS AND CRAFTS HOUSE | 139

The Dovecote

There is something familiar about the ancient market town of Bampton. Particularly its parish church, old rectory, and handsome public library—which was built as a free school in around 1650. It is because these buildings, and others, were key locations for the filming of the hit television series *Downton Abbey*, which saw Bampton stand in for the fictional Yorkshire village of Downton.

It's not hard to see why the producers chose it. Bampton is a remarkably attractive and well-preserved place. Visitors to the town, on their way to pay homage to the church where Lady Mary married Matthew Crawley, may pass an unassuming wooden door set in a high stone wall. Were they to enter, they would find themselves on a winding path leading through a secret wildflower garden, before reaching a gap in a yew hedge and a view of what is possibly the most picturesque building in the entire town.

It is a seventeenth-century dovecote with four gables rising from the centre of a Cotswold stone barn. On it sits a wooden cupola, resembling an old-fashioned beehive, topped with a fine weathervane. It is extremely pretty. "I think it looks quite French," says its owner, the famed interior decorator Emma Burns. "It reminds me of those ancient hunting lodges in the Dordogne." Painted shutters either side of French doors and the steep roofline add to the impression, as do "pigeonholes" in the gables, set there to let in doves. Emma points out the ornate hopper heads on top of the guttering that are engraved with her parents' initials.

Emma's parents bought the house when Emma was fifteen. They wanted a wreck to do up ("something to bring a vision to"), and at the time the crumbling dovecote contained loose boxes for horses, a cart in the hall, and chickens upstairs. They slowly transformed it into a liveable home with a tiny budget ("on the smell of an oily rag," as Emma puts it). They recruited the help of friends along the way, sometimes unwittingly: "My mother would invite people to lunch and then after they arrived announce, 'We're just going to lay a brick path and dismantle a pig sty.'" Emma carried on with the refurbishment when she inherited the house from them, and what she has created is testament to her skills as a decorator.

OPPOSITE: Some of the dovecote's original "pigeonholes" (now housing plastic pigeons)

Binoculars hanging on the hall stairs belonged to Emma's father, who was a great race-goer—Bampton is close to both Newbury and Cheltenham.

The dovecote has a simple layout. There are just two rooms downstairs—a kitchen and a drawing room, separated by a hall. Upstairs there are two bedrooms and a bathroom. Emma leads us through a split stable door straight into what is the epitome of a classic English country kitchen. Her parents used to have an island, but Emma took it out to make way for a large round table. She put in the stone floor to match the hallway and stripped back the ceiling to expose the joints. "It makes it look like it has always been this way."

On a windowsill, above a cream enamelled AGA oven, is a collection of Staffordshire "companion dogs." Emma loves pottery, particularly in numbers: "A lot of anything looks good, even if you don't particularly like them." There is a lineup of Wedgwood creamware jugs next to the sink. She also collects figures of people like Shakespeare and, her favourite, the great Scottish bard Robert Burns (who shares a name with her son Bobby).

The colour in the kitchen is Pimlico Green and one of a small range of paints produced by Sibyl Colefax and John Fowler, of which Emma is managing director. The company is the longest established interior decorating firm in Great Britain and one of the most respected. Emma describes her own style as "comfortable, confident, understated elegance, with a bit of frivolity." The most important thing, she says, is for a room is to be welcoming and friendly and, after that, to have some interest to it. An example is the large silver spheres hanging in the corner of the kitchen. These are "witches baubles" made by the Victorians to ward off any evil crones attempting to enter a property by distorting their faces. "I like to put things that are 'not important' into a room," says Emma. "A cracked jug with some posies will humanise a grand walnut commode." Guarding against an excess of good taste was always a tenet of the founders of Colefax and Fowler.

The kitchen leads into the hallway, which is flooded with light thanks to the extra-wide French windows (the large cavity they occupy used to house the barn doors), and on into the drawing room—"Although it's possibly a bit pretentious of me to call an old stable a drawing room," remarks Emma. Directly above is the book-filled main bedroom. In fact, there are books everywhere. "I'm always suspicious of anyone who doesn't have, or doesn't want, any books," says Emma. The landing upstairs is dedicated exclusively to classic crime authors like Dorothy L. Sayers, Agatha Christie, and Gladys Mitchell. "The reason people like crime novels," she observes, "is they are about imposing order on chaos, which is rather what interior decorating is."

Because of the limited number of rooms in the Dovecote, Emma has recently refurbished an adjoining barn. It was always used for entertaining by her parents, who would host long lunches there, but in their day, it had a

The book barn

beaten earth floor and exposed stone walls. Now it is a "book barn"—a fabulous double-height library with two galleries above, one a bedroom and one Emma's office. Downstairs, hidden behind the bookshelves, and accessed by cantilevered doors laden with books, are a bathroom and a bar cum pantry.

Outside, the garden is as artfully considered as the house. The beauty is in the detail, from giant hollyhocks to an elegant wheelbarrow, to a water butt fashioned from an old whiskey barrel ("which makes the whole garden smell like a pub"). Beyond the perfectly trimmed yew is a wildflower garden, which is dotted with standing stones. "The graves of my ex-husbands," jokes Emma; "I like to keep them close." In fact, Emma's ex-husband the recently retired MP Sir Simon Burns lives literally over the garden wall. "Which is marvellous, as it has expanded my visitor capacity quite dramatically, since he is able to have friends to stay."

Emma hasn't got a beau at the moment. "I'm dedicated to my pug." The pug in question is Dahlia, who is four years old. "She's extremely naughty and a great snob. Refuses to take public transport, and if she spots an Ugg boot, she goes berserk. She simply can't abide them." Dahlia, who is sporting a malachite collar, casts a discerning eye in our direction, as if to say there's nothing snobbish about having good taste. It's something her owner has in spades.

ABOVE: The kitchen walls are painted Pimlico Green, from a range of paints by Sibyl Colefax and John Fowler.

Wedgewood creamware jugs line up next to the kitchen sink.

RIGHT: The vintage-looking sign, "Trays for the Sands," is actually a set dressing from a television commercial that aimed to re-create a retro seaside scene.

The oil portrait on the left is of Emma's ancestor Mrs. Haddock. Her sister, a Mrs. Batty, hangs in Emma's ex-husband's kitchen next door. "Aren't they marvellous names?" says Emma.

ABOVE: The main bedroom features antique crewelwork on the bed, and walls painted in String by Farrow and Ball.

RIGHT: Upstairs in the book barn, the sleeping platform has a screen for guests to dress behind.

OPPOSITE: According to Emma, her bathroom, it turns out, "is the most Instagrammable room in the house. Whenever I post it, people go absolutely mad."

ABOVE: The glass lamps are huge green demijohns that Emma bought and had fitted as lights with shades made in a fabric by Fermoie.

LEFT: A cantilevered door in the library shelves conceals a bathroom beyond.

The two library chairs, which belonged to Emma's late partner Menno Ziessen, have been re-covered in an antique Persian jajim rug.

The room's corduroy-covered sofas were chosen because "they're like trousers—the more knackered they get, the more comfortable they become."

OPPOSITE: Looking from the drawing room into the hall. The eighteenth-century longcase clock with blue lacquer belonged to Emma's grandparents. "It lost its top," says Emma, "but I serendipitously found a little piece of glass that sits perfectly above it."

ABOVE: Above the fireplace in the drawing room are the old deeds to Bampton House (to whom the dovecote once belonged) with the seal of King George III. A pair of armchairs are covered in fabric from Antico Setificio in Florence. The parrot hanging in the far window came from Greenway Antiques in nearby Witney.

The Georgian Farmhouse

Late in the evening on the 13th of August 1705, near the banks of the River Danube in southern Bavaria, an exhausted soldier by the name of John Churchill, 1st Duke of Marlborough, pulled up his horse to scribble a quick note to his wife: "I have no time to say more but to beg you will give my duty to the Queen, and let her know her army has had a glorious victory." And so it had. Marlborough's tactical brilliance at what came to be known as the Battle of Blenheim saw more than 27,000 French soldiers killed, captured, or wounded and proved to be a turning point in the War of the Spanish Succession. It would also prove to have a profound impact on a tract of land many hundreds of miles away, in Oxfordshire, on the fringes of the Cotswolds. For when the Duke finally returned home, the queen in question (Queen Anne) bestowed upon him a large estate and a vast sum of money with which to build a suitable house in recognition of, and gratitude for, his victory. The house turned out to be a palace and was named after the battle that bought it. And the land around would be owned and farmed by generations of Churchills afterwards.

Which brings us to the gorgeous Georgian farmhouse that is Lower Whitehill Farm near Tackley. It was built as part of a model farm on what originally was part of the Blenheim estate. Though by no means grand, its original ducal owner presumably saw fit to make it "best in class," and it is as handsome as a humble farmhouse could be. Built in 1790 from coursed Cotswold stone, the two-storey house has a hipped slate roof and a symmetrical front façade with generously proportioned sash windows. An attractive open-work iron porch leads through the front door to a flagstoned hall and into the home of Vanessa Macdonald, her husband, James, and their two sons.

The Macdonalds originally spotted the house in the window of an estate agent in London and were drawn to it by its Georgian proportions, its beautiful setting, and its relative proximity to London. They attempted to buy it but were ultimately outbid. It was a disappointment, and they ended up shelving their plans to move to the countryside. But they never forgot about their dream farmhouse, and one day, some three years later, whilst visiting friends in the area, they decided to drop off a letter asking the successful bidders to consider them if they ever decided to sell. By some piece of great serendipity, the owners

OPPOSITE: Vanessa has planted Russian sage across the front façade of the house and is particularly fond of its lavender purple flowers.

ABOVE: The croquet lawn leading onto the swimming pool and the arbour beyond

OPPOSITE: Whitehill Farm house from across the valley

not only came to the door but said that they were indeed thinking of moving back to the area they had originally come from. "And so, a deal was struck," says Vanessa. "We bought it on a handshake, which was a lovely way to do it."

Vanessa is half Canadian and half Venezuelan. Coming from the jungles and waterfalls of South America and the mountains and vast landscapes of Canada, she must find the Cotswolds somewhat tame, one would think. But Vanessa has fallen for its gentle charms. "It's just so pretty. I love the rolling countryside and the colour of the stone and how ancient it all is." As she points out, Vancouver (where she grew up) is barely a century old, whereas now she is living next to the remains of a Roman road that dates back nearly two millennia, not to mention a host of nearby prehistoric settlements and ancient churches. Growing up, she was always an Anglophile: "I don't know why, but as a child I was obsessed by Spode Blue and White china and fabrics with floral patterns. And I used to subscribe to *Victoria* magazine, which was dedicated to charming homes." The farmhouse she has finally ended up living in resembles the dolls' houses of her youth.

After longing for Whitehill Farm for all those years, it was a slight shock when they finally moved in. "It was so bare and stark without furniture that we gulped." But it wasn't for long because, happily, Vanessa herself is a professional decorator who runs Melissa Wyndham Ltd—one of the UK's leading interior design practices. It was founded in 1985 by the late, legendary Melissa Wyndham. Based in Sydney Street in Chelsea, the company has decorated everything from chalets in Verbier to apartments in New York and has worked on some of the finest country houses in Britain and Ireland, including Petworth, Longleat, Chatsworth, Stowell Park, and Lismore Castle.

"The most important thing is to get the fabric of the house right—the nuts and bolts," says Vanessa. "Before you start worrying about curtains, you've got to start with the fireplaces, the floors, the skirting boards, the doors. Nine times out of ten, we are putting original features back." After that, "Comfort is key. Make sure there are tables next to chairs and sofas, sufficient lamps, and lots of books. Use an ottoman in place of a coffee table and put a lovely tray on it. It's important not to be too formal or make things too perfect. You want to create intimate spaces that look lived in."

Vanessa has applied this philosophy to Whitehill Farm, creating spaces that are elegant but lend themselves to conviviality. A club fender in front of the fire in the drawing room, for instance, gives people a place to perch on and warm their backs. She has laid sisal all over the house, "which I do for a lot of my clients in country houses," and has put rugs on top, layering textures and colours and bringing a snug comfort to the house. Vanessa mixes traditional

Persians with contemporary designs, many from her own collection at Melissa Wyndham.

The Macdonalds love to entertain, and their geniality as hosts continues into the gardens around the house. There are multiple areas in which to sit and eat. They have a croquet lawn and have built a swimming pool overlooked by an arbour. They even persuaded the local farmer to sell them an acre of the nearest field so they could create a cricket pitch, where their boys organise matches amongst their friends. It's extraordinary to think that a bloody war fought three hundred years ago could have contributed to such a place of peace and happiness today.

OVERLEAF: The portrait above the sitting room fireplace is of Vanessa's sons, painted by Luke Martineau. "I love to put my feet up on a stool, so much better than a coffee table—especially in the country."

The rug on the floor is from a Melissa Wyndham collection in collaboration with Robert Stephenson.

The room is painted in calming Farrow and Ball Old White.

A television is hidden under the cloth of a round table in the corner. "Very old-school—but my husband insists on it," says Vanessa.

LEFT: The drawing room is painted Farrow and Ball French Grey. The curtain fabric is from Christopher Moore, and the carpet is from Robert Stephenson. A Cornish seascape over the fireplace reminds the family of their annual pilgrimage to St. Mawes in Cornwall.

A horsehair-covered fender is from Acres Farm.

Vanessa installed a new fireplace, which is from Jamb on Pimlico Road.

ABOVE: A view from the flagstoned front hall into the sitting room. The antique "boot jack" leaning against the wall aids in the removal of boots.

Vanessa's antique writing desk in the sitting room. The chair is by Julian Chichester. The vase is from Cutter Brooks.

OPPOSITE: Vanessa's bedroom. The headboard is covered in a fabric called Mughal Flower, by Robert Kime. It is a particular favourite of Vanessa's, and she has used it in several places in the house.

ABOVE: The en suite bathroom is painted in Light Blue by Farrow and Ball. The chair fabric is buy Christopher Moore. "I always try to use an upholstered chair in a bathroom if space permits, as it makes the room feel less functional and more comfortable, especially in a country house," says Vanessa.

OPPOSITE TOP: The dining room is part of the open-plan kitchen. The antique cupboard is from Ardgowan Antiques; the wall lights are Charles Edwards, and the storm candles are Collier Webb.

OPPOSITE BOTTOM LEFT: The kitchen is painted in Farrow and Ball Old White. Vanessa loves the classic AGA oven, which came with the house, but in an ideal world would actually prefer it to be white rather than cream.

OPPOSITE BOTTOM RIGHT: The flagstoned floor in the hall is original to the house. The lantern is from Howe London.

ABOVE: Vanessa has lined the guest cottage's sitting room walls with painted wooden boards and has embraced a more rustic look than in the main house. The boat is antique. The feather lampshade is made by Claire Henman.

RIGHT: Vanessa designed the mirror in the guest bathroom and had it made. The lampshade fabric is from Robert Kime. The panelling is painted in Cerulean Blue from Edward Bulmer.

The Village House

I must confess to a particular soft spot for the village of Meysey Hampton. My children spent their early school years there. And during that period, I had a happy time attending plays and concerts in the village hall, at candlelit carol services in the ancient church, and watching the children dance around a Maypole on the village green to celebrate the start of summer (the school's headmistress was a great traditionalist). It is a delightful village in a bucolic setting.

I'm not alone in finding the village charming. In 1931, the ruralist writer and poet H. J. Massingham described Meysey Hampton as a "naturally gracious village inlaid into so pastoral a landscape and so embowered in flowers that it surely would be spirited away at a touch of the Machine Age." Mercifully, it hasn't been spirited away, and although nearly a century has passed since he wrote those words, Meysey Hampton remains largely unencroached upon by modernity.

In the very centre of the village, within a feeble throw of a pebble from the village green, is Meysey Hampton Manor. Sitting behind high Cotswold stone walls and in two acres of beautiful grounds, it is the perfect village house, with many of the hallmarks of a classic Cotswold manor. Its elegant and spacious rooms date principally from the early sixteenth century, but the house was enlarged and gentrified in the mid-eighteenth century with a classical Georgian façade.

An early occupant is thought to have been the famous physician and surgeon James Vaulx, a memorial to whom can be found in nearby St. Mary's Church. Dr. Vaulx's reputation in Stuart Britain was so great that James I considered making him his royal physician, but upon asking the great doctor how he obtained his knowledge of the healing art, he was alarmed by Vaulx's reply: "By practice." The king rejoined, "Then by my soul thou hast killed many a man, thou shall na' practise upon me." Perhaps this royal rejection contributed to the slightly miserable figure that the doctor cuts in his effigy in St. Mary's. He is seen leaning heavily upon a skull, with his head in his hand. He looks exhausted, as well he might, as the monument reveals that he had two wives and sixteen children.

The manor house today is owned by Paul Tabor and Julie Gad. It was something of an impulse buy for them. The couple were spending a weekend

OPPOSITE: The Georgian main façade of Meysey Hampton Manor

The urn came with the house. "We can put our ashes in there when we pop our clogs," says Paul. "It's large enough to fit us all, including the dogs."

in the Cotswolds, and Paul had booked a couple of properties to look at, just for fun, although they had no real plans to leave their life in London. But as soon they drove through the gates and saw the beautiful stone house and its pretty accompanying barns, they were enraptured.

The house was more work than they envisaged. "We thought we would be spending all our money on the aesthetic, but actually it was the structure that needed the most work." New timbers in the roof were required, along with new floorboards through much of the house, new stairs, and more. They also reconfigured the house somewhat, particularly upstairs. There were originally eight bedrooms, but the house now has only four, as Paul and Julie wanted to create private spaces for themselves and their daughters. So each of them now has a luxuriously appointed bedroom, with a dressing room and bathroom en suite.

In terms of interior decoration, Julie took the lead. She has always decorated her own homes. Being Danish, she brings a definite Scandinavian feel to her rooms. She is fond of cool tones and calm spaces. She mixes her own paint colours in what Paul jokingly calls "Fifty Thousand Shades of Grey," but on top of this neutral background both she and Paul have a great appetite for texture and modern and contemporary art. So the house is full of colour and interesting paintings and sculptures. Every room also contains fabulous collections of dried flowers, branches, and found objects from the natural world. Julie is heavily influenced by the famous Danish florist and artist Tage Andersen, who was a great friend of her parents.

On entering the house one is greeted by a ten-foot-tall stuffed polar bear. Paul and Julie bought it at a party at Aynhoe Park—the Grade I party palace previously owned by the eccentric collector James Perkins. Julie dresses it according to the season. On the day we visit, it is sporting a top hat and holding a giant sprig of gypsophila (also known as baby's breath). It sets the tone for the rest of the house and speaks of its owners' fun and eclectic tastes.

There are three main rooms housed in the Georgian part of the house: a large kitchen with dining area, a formal drawing room with a matching pair of French eighteenth-century fireplaces, and a library. The library, though, is dedicated more to music than to books, as it houses Paul's collection of vinyl records.

All of these rooms look out onto a stone flagged terrace and a large lawn beyond. The gardens are heavenly. "Spring is absolutely spectacular here," says Julie. "The main lawn is covered in hundreds of snowdrops, which are replaced by crocuses, which are replaced by daffodils." There are two flowering tulip trees. And the orchard, which contains apples, pears, quince, crab apples, and plums, is a riot of blossom in April and May.

At the back of the house is a tennis court and a swimming pool. The whole family likes to keep fit, but it is the cairn terrier, Storm, who seems to make most use of the pool. "He keeps jumping in and doing lengths," says Paul. "The dog hair in the filter drives me mad!" But he can't help but smile. The couple indulge all their four dogs. Otto, an adorable miniature dachshund, is allowed to cross the kitchen table at breakfast and lick the foam off Paul's cappuccino.

From the top of the house there are views across the stone roofs of the village to the fields beyond. Two miles South from Meysey Hampton is the Old Rectory, where Ralph Vaughan Williams, one of England's most celebrated composers, was born. Vaughan Williams's most famous work, *The Lark Ascending*, is a highly romantic piece that describes the flight of a songbird, depicted by a violin, as it soars over a pastoral landscape. It is an exquisite piece of music that is both a hymn to the grace and joy of the little bird and a tribute to this most idyllic corner of the Cotswolds.

The heart hanging over the coach house door comes from Daylesford.

This library is also used as a music room. Paul keeps a record player here for listening to his vinyl collection, in a mirrored cabinet with cognac-coloured glass.

The wood burner is similar to a giant version that Paul and Julie fell in love with at a hotel in Portugal.

The photos above the fireplace are by Maryam Eisler.

ABOVE: The drawing room is bookended by a pair of fireplaces from Simon Wharton. They are French and mid-eighteenth-century—the same period as this part of the house.

OPPOSITE TOP: Julie chose the burnt-orange velvet for the drawing room sofa because it reminded her of a Jaipur sunset. The lips photograph is by Miles Aldridge, the famous fashion photographer.

OPPOSITE BOTTOM LEFT: Paul's blue weimaraner, Pablo, in the front hall. Paul had long hankered after a big dog, "but I had to find one that matched the house."

OPPOSITE BOTTOM RIGHT: The staircase was reputedly designed by Sir John Soane.

The baby grand piano at its base is ornamental. None of the family can play, but it is kept tuned: "If a friend comes round who can play, it is an absolute joy."

The chandelier above the staircase is from Lorford Antiques.

ABOVE: The bedroom of Julie's oldest daughter, Tashia, has very clean lines, floating cabinetry, and a beautiful view of the adjoining coach house.

BELOW: Paul and Julie's bathroom

OPPOSITE: The main bedroom suite occupies the entire first floor of the Georgian front and houses a contemporary four-poster bed by Simon Horn.

ABOVE: The wrought-iron light over the dining table is frequently styled by Julie with different flowers and coloured candles to match the table settings. The floor is made from aged ash from Holland.

A verdigris egg on the windowsill is by Tage Andersen—who was a friend of Julie's parents.

OPPOSITE TOP: The kitchen cabinets, including the island with the antique legs and claw and ball feet, were designed by Julie and made by Heartwood Designs. The lamps are from Nicholas Haslam in Holbein Place.

OPPOSITE BOTTOM: Carrara marble tiles behind the oven, with an eighteenth-century fireback in front. The domed skylights in the ceiling throw an attractive light into the room.

The Hotchpotch

*A*rriving at Farmhill Park, one feels instantly at home. Is it the warmth of the wood burning stove in the seventeenth-century hall? Is it the smell from the Moka coffeepot bubbling away on the AGA top in the kitchen? Is it the enthusiastic greeting from the two waggy-tailed spaniels? Or is it the glimpse through into the drawing room, which is full of squashy sofas and contains one of the largest and most exotically stocked drinks tables I've ever seen? It is, of course, all of these things and more. And it comes as no surprise, for this is the home of Sam and Georgie Pearman, two consummate hosts who over the past fifteen years have created some of the most feted pubs, hotels, and restaurants in the Cotswolds.

The Pearmans co-founded the Lucky Onion group and created No. 131—the super-chic townhouse hotel in Cheltenham—and the iconic pub the Wheatsheaf in Northleach. In 2017 they branched out on their own, and they now have three pubs cum hotels under their Country Creatures moniker—the Chequers in Churchill, the Swan in Ascott-under-Wychwood, and the Double Red Duke in Clanfield. All are famed for their exquisite food, their stylish design, and the warmth of their welcome.

The couple didn't start out in hospitality, however. In their twenties, Georgie was a city lawyer who specialised in mergers and acquisitions, and Sam was a professional rugby player for Gloucester and Scotland. When their first child, Lily, reached school age, and with Georgie tiring of the law, they grabbed a chance to move to the Cotswolds and help a friend run the then Bibury Court Hotel. It was a giant leap of faith, but they both had a deep love of the countryside and they knew the area well. Sam has relations in Stow-on-the-Wold, and Georgie spent her early childhood on the northern fringes of the Cotswolds, near Broadway.

Farmhill Park is what Georgie describes as a "classic Cotswold hotchpotch" that bears the imprint of the different families and generations who have lived here and their rising and falling fortunes. Its central core, which downstairs incorporates what is now the entrance hall and Sam's study, was built sometime in the 1600s. Fabulous stained glass from this period—depicting local fauna—still exists in in the windows on the staircase. Large Victorian extensions on either side have been extended upon themselves. Arts and Crafts additions from the early twentieth century include the fire surround in the hall, which has an

OPPOSITE: The central bay of Farmhill Park is the earliest part of the house, dating back to the 1600s.

ABOVE: Georgie's spaniel outside the back door of the house

OPPOSITE: The Arts and Crafts fireplace in the entrance hall. Two giant log baskets keep the wood burner well stocked, ensuring guests a warm welcome.

inscription elegantly carved into its mantel that reads "East, West, Home's Best." And so it is, for what stands today is a sizable and extremely comfortable family home—a home, appropriately for the Pearmans, that is perfect for entertaining. The generously proportioned reception rooms include a formal dining room which, at Christmas, can seat up to twenty-four people. There are ten bedrooms split between the two floors above, each named after an English cathedral city. Many of the bathrooms have freestanding baths looking out over the gardens below. In the drawing room, an old-fashioned record player sits near the aforementioned drinks table. Sam, whose cocktail menus are much admired, is obviously the family mixologist. "I just drink what I'm given," says Georgie, "and it's always something delicious."

Farmhill sits hidden in a hollow on the side of a hill on the outskirts of Stroud. This bustling market town in the centre of Gloucestershire was recently named by a national newspaper as the best place to live in the entire United Kingdom. Quite an accolade. Georgie loves its community spirit and its fantastic food scene. Her own cousin Noni has recently set up an eponymous ethical coffee roastery there, and Georgie's daughters love to go to the town's famous Saturday farmers' market. It has always been a magnet for artists, musicians, writers, hippies, healers, and political revolutionaries. In recent years it has become a stronghold of the green movement. Extinction Rebellion was founded here, and the local football team Forest Green Rovers is the world's first carbon-neutral football club and has a ground that sells only vegan food. This free-thinking, radical spirit stretches back centuries, and Farmhill Park has at times been at the centre of it. Just below the house today is a triumphant arch celebrating the abolition of slavery in 1833—the only one of its kind in the UK—built by proud local abolitionist Henry Wyatt, the owner of the original Farmhill estate.

The only slight cloud over this supremely welcoming home is the Pearmans' cat, Sour, whose name fits his demeanour. Outraged by the arrival of the family's new puppy, Sour has taken to living in a cupboard in the kitchen and stares at us with unbridled disgust when we peek into his new, self-appointed quarters. Sam, normally the most genial of hosts, wonders why he doesn't just move out altogether, before sheepishly admitting, "I'm definitely more of a dog person." But Sourpuss aside, life in Stroud is pretty sweet.

The drawing room is painted in French Grey by Farrow and Ball.

ABOVE: The horses sign in Georgie's office comes from a circus. Georgie bought it from Archie Mackie at Original House. The cushions on the sofa were made up from old Indian fabric; the woodwork is painted in Pigeon by Farrow and Ball.

OPPOSITE TOP: An eclectic collection of art, from movie posters to Russian prints to original oil paintings, hangs in the kitchen.

OPPOSITE BOTTOM: The classic AGA cooker "is really just a very expensive radiator" (there is a conventional oven in the ancillary kitchen next-door). Georgie is suspicious of it, as you can put something in it and forget about it: "As you can't see or smell anything, you can sometimes just discover the carbonized remains days later."

LEFT TOP: The main picture above the bed is of one of Sam's parents' racehorses, painted in the 1980s.

LEFT BOTTOM: Georgie was delighted by the bath in the window of the master en suite, which came with the house.

OPPOSITE: An oak Arts and Crafts low cabinet, inherited from Georgie's grandmother, stands in the hall. The framed magazines above it are a vintage French publication called *Lyon*, some dating to the nineteenth century. "I bought bundles of them from the market near my parents' house in France," says Georgie.

ABOVE LEFT: The sideboard was inherited from Sam's parents. The prints above it were bought at Christie's and are part of a collection called "I'm telling you stories, trust me," whereby a selection of artists were commissioned to produce works based on that title.

ABOVE RIGHT: The huge table in the dining room is surrounded by contemporary chairs from Belgium.

OPPOSITE: The vast drinks table in the drawing room is an old industrial piece from Archie Mackie.

Cottage Industry

The Cotswolds is classic hunting country and home to some of the greatest packs of foxhounds in England: the Heythrop, the Duke of Beaufort's, the Vale of the White Horse, the North Cotswold, and others. The vales, valleys, and woods provide exhilarating sport for the keen horsemen and women of the region. These hunts all have pony clubs attached and point-to-points (amateur races over jumps) and all manner of social engagements. And with all this horsing around comes lots of fabulous clothing: cavalry twill frock coats, hacking jackets, tattersall waistcoats, pink tailcoats for hunt balls, tweed suits for racing, and the like. In 1904, to cater to the clothing needs of the area's hunting and racing types, the tailors Smith and Hobbs set up a workshop in the tiny village of Woodmancote, near North Cerney. They built a corrugated-iron shed that for the next eighty years hummed with the sound of sewing machines and a team of seamstresses busy at their work.

This "tin shed," as its current owner, Archie Mackie, refers to it, is now the annex to Tally Cottage—which possibly takes its name from the traditional cry of "Tally-ho" made by a huntsman to alert the rest of the field that a quarry had been sighted. The cottage itself dates back to around 1750. Built from Cotswold stone rubble with mullioned windows and a stone tiled roof, it is a fetching example of Cotswold vernacular architecture.

Archie and his wife, Caddy, bought it in the mid-2000s. They loved the cosiness of the cottage with its thick walls, two large fireplaces, and low ceilings. To Archie, it had a slightly Cornish impression and reminded him of fishermen's cottages in Fowey on the South Coast, near to where he grew up. The kitchen in particular, with its exposed timbers, feels rather like a ship's galley.

They were also attracted by the village. "Woodmancote is a lovely working village," says Archie. "No weekenders. Everyone knows everyone. When you go for drinks at someone's house, the whole community is there." He knew that it would be a happy place to bring up their three children, and so it has proved. "When it snows in the winter the whole village goes sledging together en masse

OPPOSITE: Tally Cottage

OPPOSITE: The former tailor's workshop, with its "tin" cladding

on a hill over the way." In the summer, a walnut tree in the garden is used for climbing and den-building, and the children play croquet and badminton and splash about in a paddling pool.

But as well as all this, Archie saw great potential in the shed. He wanted the opportunity to renovate something and was attracted by such a large, open space.

When they first moved in, the old workshop was "knackered," untouched for forty years. The paint on the roof was flaking off and the interior was still full of old Singer sewing machines and dusty bales of cloth. At first the kids used it as indoor tricycle track, but gradually Archie began to restore it. As it was a designated place of historical interest, he needed to preserve its original appearance. So he hired a local specialist, "Tin Mitch," to strip off the old cladding and replace it with new corrugated iron. He then remade the corner finials, restoring the shed to how it must have looked when it was first erected. Inside, Archie shot-blasted the pine walls, with a view to then finishing them, but liked the patina so much he left them and painted the floor instead.

Archie built the kitchen himself with copper handles made out of old plumbing fixtures. "I decided I wanted a splash of copper running throughout the building." To that end he installed vintage sand-cast copper light switches (which are made by pouring molten copper into sand moulds) and hung two huge copper lights from the ceiling. These 1950s industrial pendants from Hungary were originally enamelled, but Archie shot blasted them and coated them in copper.

At one end of the building Archie has created a bedroom and bathroom for guests, but the rest of the shed he has left open plan, partly because he liked the idea of a large, fun entertaining area and partly because he wanted a clean, contemporary space to showcase pieces of furniture from the company that he and Caddy run together. Original House, which they founded, sells vintage and industrial furniture and lighting alongside decorative antiques. But Archie particularly favours early twentieth-century industrial pieces, like workbenches and factory lights, objects that were built with utility in mind rather than decoration but have a strong aesthetic appeal, nevertheless.

Archie fell into this world having studied product design at university. After his studies he ended up working for a famous reclamation company in London and fell in love with turning salvaged items into decorative objects. And these vintage objects work perfectly against the backdrop of the restored workshop. It lends itself to fun parties, with its long dining room table and plenty of space for dancing (although Archie, who is a keen amateur mixologist, sheepishly admits, "I generally hide behind the bar"). Tally-ho, indeed!

ABOVE: The tongue-and-groove back wall is painted in Farrow and Ball's Railings, to match the kitchen units. The "Chemist" sign is from a shop in Bembridge on the Isle of Wight and dates from around 1910.

The 1930s burnished steel industrial sideboard is from Paris.

LEFT: The interior of the shed. The Texas longhorn skull is from Albuquerque, New Mexico.

ABOVE: The bedside lights in the guest bedroom come from an ocean liner.

OPPOSITE: The pink bathroom is painted in Paint and Paper Library's Rhubarb. The vintage sink was a bargain find on Etsy.

ABOVE: In the kitchen is a window seat shaped to fit the curved wall and covered with grey wool.

RIGHT: The sitting room coffee table is an old foundry trolley. The green log baskets are old grape harvesting baskets from France that would have been worn on the pickers' backs. Sometimes you find them with the chateau's name painted on.

A painting of Ithaca in Greece, titled *The Walk to Helena's Church*, is by Christopher Johnson; nearby, a cut down pommel horse makes a perfect fireside perch.

ABOVE AND RIGHT: Archie converted a small outhouse into a boot room (aka mud room) and used the same tongue-and-groove panelling as in the shed.

OPPOSITE: The kitchen terrace

The Stately Home

What is a "stately home"? The expression was first coined by the early nineteenth-century poet Felicia Dorothea Hemans:

The stately homes of England
How beautiful they stand!
Amidst their tall ancestral trees,
O'er all the pleasant land!

The poem was later parodied by Noël Coward:

The Stately Homes of England,
How beautiful they stand,
To prove the upper classes
Have still the upper hand;
Though the fact that they have to be rebuilt
And frequently mortgaged to the hilt
Is inclined to take the gilt
Off the gingerbread . . .

Coward was right about two things: They were built as fabulous status symbols, and, more often than not, their fortunes have declined alongside those of the aristocratic families who originally commissioned them. These impressive houses were built throughout the British Isles, although many have been lost over the years to fire or have been pulled down due to the ruinous cost of their upkeep. Surviving examples must now earn their keep and are commonly open to the public (often through institutions like the National Trust and the English Heritage).

Bruern Abbey is perhaps not an ideal example. It is not open to the public. And whilst it is certainly a grand and beautiful country house that was built to impress, its scale is far more modest than the behemoths we usually associate with the term. As a "small stately," though, it is ideal; for who needs hundreds of rooms when you can have a handful of perfect ones?

OPPOSITE: The classical south façade of Bruern Abbey, built in 1720

The house takes its name from a Cistercian Abbey that was founded on the site in 1147. The monks who lived here seemed somewhat unruly, and the records from the period detail quarrels, plots, financial irregularities, punishments for lying, deposed abbots, and more. When Henry VIII dissolved the monastery in 1536, the locals were probably rather relieved to see the back of such a dissolute lot. The estate eventually found its way into the hands of the Cope family, and in around 1720 the house as we know it today was built by Sir John Cope. Or, at least, the main south façade as we know it today was built; the rest of the house burnt down in 1780 and was rebuilt with new wings. Bruern's Victorian owners made further additions, which in turn were pulled down when the house was remodelled by its then owner, Michael Astor (son of the 2nd Viscount Astor and his wife, Nancy), in the 1970s. What Astor left, in footprint at least, was probably a fair approximation of the original English baroque building. And what a building it is. The seven-bay front with keystoned windows underneath a classical pediment is elegance personified. It is reputed to have been designed by a local architect who worked alongside Sir John Vanbrugh on nearby Blenheim Palace.

In the late 1980s the house was turned into a successful school that eventually outgrew it and moved on. Its current owners are Lord Glendonbrook (previously Sir Michael Bishop) and Martin Ritchie. The couple acquired the property after spotting it online from their home in Australia. They had been searching for an English country house for a couple of years and specifically wanted something classically beautiful in the Georgian style that was in easy reach of London. Bruern fitted the bill, and both were smitten by the photographs of the façade but somewhat daunted by its apparent size. They asked a friend who lived in the area to check it out on their behalf, and he reported back that it seemed more manageable than one might imagine, so they jumped on a plane back to the UK to view it and bought it on sight.

Lord Glendonbrook and Martin's main job was to "de-institutionalise" the place, as it still retained vestiges of its days as a school. They then set about refurbishing the house to their exacting standards. The whole roof came off the lower ranges, and rotten dormers were rebuilt. The existing main staircase from the 1970s was replaced with a sweeping, curved structure hewn from Portland stone. A new kitchen was created on the west side of the house and new bathrooms put next to every one of the eight bedrooms. The whole house was re-wired and re-plumbed and made fit for the twenty-first century, with more than twenty-five kilometres of data cabling alone. At its peak there were more than eighty workers on the project, many of whom were living in a temporary village they created in the grounds. As a result, the house was finished within eighteen months of breaking ground. What the couple have created perfectly preserves the Georgian integrity of the building whilst making it supremely comfortable for contemporary living.

When it came to interior decoration, the new owners wanted a period style for the house but "without it looking like your maiden aunt lives here." The couple, who have been together for thirty-seven years, had quite a lot of furniture from their previous houses but had to buy more to fill Bruern. As much as possible they tried to buy early Georgian pieces from a similar period to the house. They have also hung a lot of oil paintings that would have been in keeping with the sort of art that a wealthy family like the Copes would have been buying in the eighteenth century on grand tours of Europe.

They recruited the help of two separate interior designers, Grant White during the refurbishment and subsequently Diana Sieff. "On a project of this size you have to be both bold and trusting," says Lord Glendonbrook. "You can't agonise over every decision; you need to be quick."

At the very start of the project, they also hired a garden designer. "We knew we had to start work on the gardens immediately; we couldn't wait for the house to be done first." They were recommended Angel Collins, who is based in Warwickshire. She was delighted to take on the six acres of garden. "It was a wonderful canvas, but quite daunting," admits Angel, "but Lord Glendonbrook gave me the best brief possible when he told me to 'keep it simple.'" In terms of structure, it is simple, with a symmetrical layout and repeating patterns that reflect the formality of the baroque exterior of the house. The complexity and detail come in the planting. What Angel has created is stunning. The gardens are already much feted by the likes of the Royal Horticultural Society, and garden enthusiasts from all over the world have been to visit on private tours. And it is not just the formality they are charmed by, but some of Angel's quirkier touches as well. She has created a beautiful wildflower meadow, for instance, on top of the roof of the large hidden garage that houses Martin's collection of classic English cars.

On the evening before our visit, Lord Glendonbrook and Martin had taken one of these cars, a Jaguar E-type, for a spin to a favourite local pub—the King's Head in Bledington. This pub is run by a friend of theirs, Archie Orr-Ewing, who also captains Bruern's cricket team—a side that plays on a beautiful field near to the house. Lord Glendonbrook and Martin happily encourage its upkeep for the sheer pleasure of hearing leather on willow on summer evenings. The sort of evening when they wander through the garden to the end of the canal. "We take our gin and tonics and sit on the bench at the end," says Martin, "and we look back at the house and pinch ourselves. Can we really be living here?"

ABOVE: The view from the drawing room over the front lawn

OVERLEAF LEFT: An ornamental lake (called "the Canal") is situated in front of the main façade of the house.

OVERLEAF RIGHT TOP: The cloisters in the courtyard were very useful when the house was a school, as pupils hurried from the science labs to their dorms.

OVERLEAF RIGHT BOTTOM: Bruern Abbey's spectacular garden, created by Angel Collins

ABOVE: A view from the drawing room through to the music room

LEFT: The fabric-covered walls of the Gallery Hall bring warmth and an acoustic softness to the room.

A late eighteenth-century gilded Scandinavian wall clock by Joshua Nyberg hangs on the south wall. There are clocks throughout the house. "Some of our friends are driven mad by the ticking, but we love the look and sound of them," says Martin.

ABOVE AND RIGHT: This double-aspect sitting room is called the Music Room, as that is originally what it was. The hand-mixed, dragged green paint was done by the specialist decorator Johnny Brunson.

The pugilist painting is by the celebrated Argentinian artist Jorge Larco (1897–1967).

There are small oil paintings of Venetian scenes in the corner of the room.

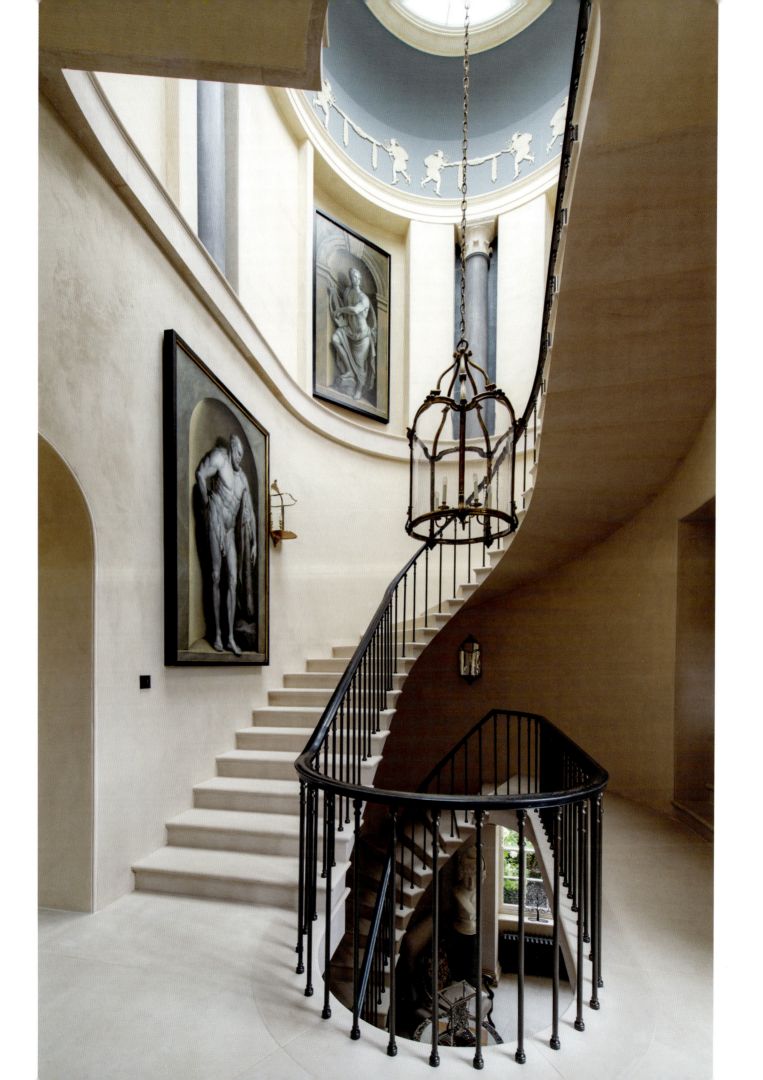

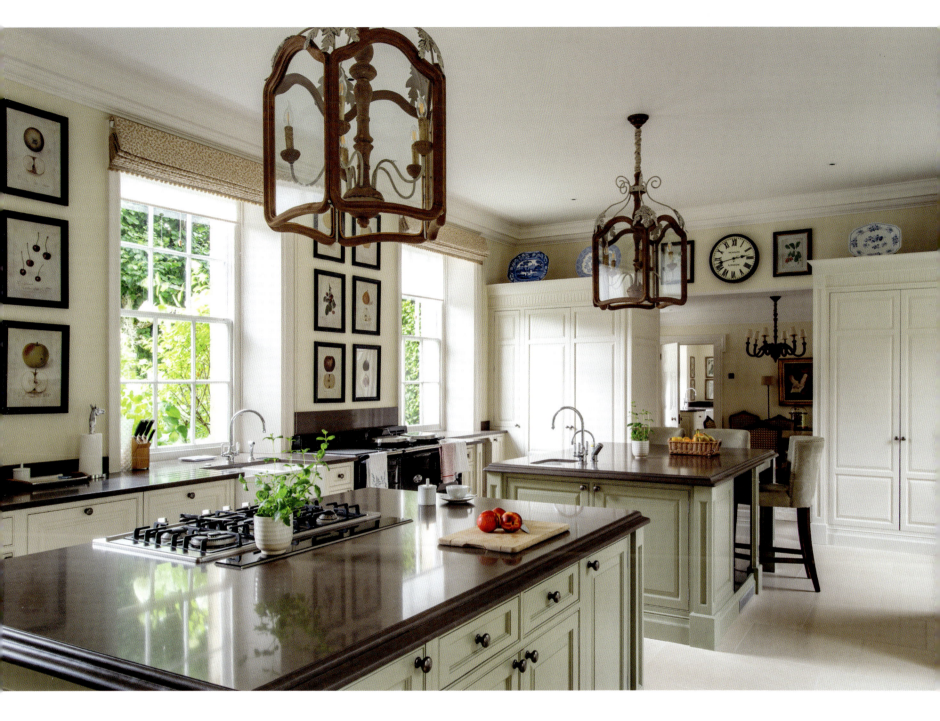

OPPOSITE: The design of the blue and white frieze at the top of the staircase mimics the Wedgwood panels of the best guest bedroom and features Mercury holding a propellor, as a nod to Lord Glendonbrook's career in aviation (he owned the airline BMI).

The classical pictures hanging on the staircase were bought from another great Cotswold "stately," Bathurst Park in Cirencester.

ABOVE: Granite tops of the two islands in the kitchen. OKA floral prints are on the walls. The black AGA came with the house but was repositioned between the windows on the west wall.

ABOVE: The candlestick on the overmantel depicts a crane standing on a tortoise—an ancient image from Chinese mythology, symbolising good luck and longevity.

LEFT: The principal guest bedroom, looking out over the front lawn of the house

ABOVE: A vaulted bedroom in one of the lower ranges of the house. The ornate bedhead was designed by Grant White.

RIGHT: Antique maps of Britain hang on the walls of the bathroom. Cleverly, the glass walls of the shower incorporate one of the roof beams.

OPPOSITE: The media room, which contains a drum kit, keyboard, and Martin's collection of guitars, used to be a dormitory in the days when the house was a school. You can still see some schoolboy graffiti carved into the beams. A 1960s Rock-Ola jukebox sits at one end and plays an eclectic mix of music, from George Formby to Ultravox. There is a Richard Serra circle painting on the back wall.

Paradise

Cath Kidston lives in Paradise, quite literally. Her house lies within a tiny hamlet of that name, which takes its title from the picturesque and perfectly named Paradise Valley, in which it sits. It is an impossibly romantic setting on the outskirts of Painswick—a particularly charming town known as "the Queen of the Cotswolds." During the civil war the Royalist army was encamped here for a night, and legend has it that King Charles I climbed to the top of Painswick Beacon and, seeing the beautiful valley to the east, said, "This must be Paradise."

The house itself is as heavenly as its setting. Parts of it date back to the fifteenth century, but the front façade was put on in 1730 in a charming, late-baroque style that eschews formal Palladian rules. The site itself is prehistoric and likely to have been continually occupied by humans for the past two and a half thousand years. It was once the entrance to an Iron Age fort on Painswick Hill.

The current house sits on an ancient motte, with steps leading down from the front to what would have been a carriage drive. Like so many of the houses in this book, the building bears the imprint of the different generations who lived here. The front porch is an Edwardian addition, for instance. And the pointed gothic glazing to the sash windows was an early nineteenth-century piece of flamboyance by the house's then owner, who also built a castellated round tower on the north side of the house.

Cath and her husband, Hugh, bought the house ten years ago. They previously had a house in the idyllic Slad Valley—made famous by Laurie Lee, who described his childhood there in his autobiographical novel *Cider with Rosie*. It was traditionally Cotswolds with mullioned windows and a steep staircase, and the couple loved it, but, as Cath explains, "I know it sounds very spoilt, but I was brought up in an eighteenth-century house with sash windows and always hankered after them." Then one day they spotted a house advertised for sale in *Country Life* magazine and fell in love with its tall Georgian windows. They immediately went to see it. "It was a miserable, rainy day, but despite the gloomy weather the house was still so light, and that's what sold it to us."

Cath Kidston is extremely well known as a designer who set up a home furnishings and fashion business that, at its peak, had stores all over the world. Interior decoration has always been her great love. Her first job was working for

OPPOSITE: The sundial below the pediment of the front façade is inscribed with the Latin phrase *Pereunt et imutantur* ("The days we waste will be charged to us.")

the legendary decorator Nicky Haslam. "He gave me so much confidence and, importantly, made me realise that work could be something creative and fun."

Cath is the granddaughter of the dashing war hero and racing car driver Glen "Lucky" Kidston. She was once standing in front of one of her shops at Heathrow Airport when a passer-by stopped and looked up at her name on the front and said, "If you think she's something, you should look up her grandfather." Lucky Kidston fought in the First World War at the age of just fifteen and got his nickname after surviving accidents in aeroplanes, motorcycles, speedboats, and even submarines. Cath says, "If things ever get tough, I think if I have just five per cent of Glen in me, I will be okay. So, I think I am a bit brave."

She needed a bit of that bravery when she and Hugh bought the house in Paradise. The roof needed re-doing, and the whole house needed to be re-plumbed and re-wired. She then had to decorate the substantial ten-bedroom home. "Decorating is complicated. I can spend hours decorating a table, for instance, but at the same time the last thing I want is to make things look too precious, too considered." Hugh is happy to leave her to it. "The only thing he insists on is large televisions, which are a bit of an eyesore—I'm planning on covering one with a tapestry."

The most striking thing about the house is Cath's love of colour. She is the antithesis of minimalist interior decorators who favour neutral palettes. Her largest guest bedroom, for example, is a riot of reds, oranges, and pinks. "I was leafing through some books and came across a bedroom done by John Fowler with pale pink curtains and a red bed and decided to do something similar but add in orange."

And she adds colour to existing things, like the striking blue top of the drinks table in the hall. It was an old table of Cath's parents for which she had the painted-glass top specially cut. "The hall could be quite serious without funky elements like that," says Cath.

She also has a great sense of fun. A large portrait of a gentleman in the hall was bought to go with a painting of a Dutch woman that she inherited from her aunt. "One year we used a paper hat from a Christmas cracker to cover his bald head, and I've kept it there, as it gives him a jaunty air."

One of the guest bedrooms is called the Fish Room, after the large aquatic painting in its adjoining bathroom. It was originally a theatrical backdrop which Cath found in an antiques shop on Lillie Road in West London. "I bought it with a bathroom in mind and then based the bedroom around it."

The bathroom is a mixture of practicality and luxury and, importantly for Cath, is "timeless." She put white linoleum on the floor "because it is so

simple, clean, and cheap" but then surrounded an old bath with marble and installed a vintage loo. "I don't want anyone to be able to date the house as to when I did it up," says Cath. And one can't, because every room mixes antique furniture with new, old-fashioned chintz alongside bold, modern fabrics and contemporary art next to ancestral portraits. "Too much good taste without a little eccentricity is boring," says Cath. "You need some ugly next to pretty; otherwise, things get bland." The result is a home that is brilliantly stylish yet remains faithful to its centuries-old origins as a grand country house. It is a veritable piece of paradise.

ABOVE: Sitting on a painted table in the entrance hall is a sculpture by Ivan Black, which moves with the breeze when the front door is open. Above the table is a charcoal drawing of a giant oak tree in Richmond by Roy Wright.

LEFT: A blazing fire welcomes guests into the front hall. The pictures above the fireplace are by the Turner Prize–winning artist Chris Ofili, who is best known for his paintings incorporating elephant dung. The yellow sculpture on the pine chest is by John Buck.

ABOVE: The drawing room contains old Howard sofas in their original colours. The branch above the fireplace is by Dan Chadwick and is cast in bronze.

RIGHT: Cath bought the elephant stools from Lillie Road in West London, which is famous for its antiques shops. "Half of my furniture comes from there."

LEFT: Cath didn't want the dining room to be too formal, "since we eat in here all the time—as soon as we are more than six people." The red chairs are by the antiques dealer and furniture designer Christopher Howe. Cath designed the wallpaper herself for her new company, Joy of Print: "I think paper makes a room less formal." The fun cockerel lamp is from Tetbury: "I adore white china lamps. I have all manner of dogs and pineapples." Cath loves to play with table settings. The pink rimmed table mats come from Casa Lopez. The wool curtains are from the Yorkshire textile specialist AW Hainsworth.

BELOW: Around the fireplace in the telly room is a club fender covered in blue horsehair. Above the fire is a portrait of Sir John Astley, one of Cath's ancestors.

RIGHT: The drinks table has a specially cut painted glass top. The huge wicker basket under the table is full of mixers. Cath encourages her guests to help themselves and make their own drinks. The marbled lampshade is by Rosi de Ruig.

OPPOSITE: Cath buys a lot of books, particularly biographies, and has also inherited some, including her late brother's Anthony Powell collection. Above the bookcase is an Anthony Buck sculpture.

The table is from Heals, in a great "nail polish red" colour. On it sits a Lynn Chadwick bronze of a couple on a bench, which Hugh bought before he met Cath.

"I like putting mirrors in places where you don't actually have to look at yourself, where they reflect more interesting things than one's own face, like books or flowers," says Cath.

ABOVE: The prints above the bed are by Henrietta Molinaro. "I saw them in blue and white and asked if she'd do them in red."

The needlework cushions are made by prisoners, organised by a charity called Fine Cell Work, of which Cath is a trustee.

OPPOSITE TOP LEFT AND BOTTOM: This bedroom is known as "the Fish Room" because of the large aquatic painting in its adjoining bathroom.

OPPOSITE TOP RIGHT: The fish painting that dominates the bathroom was originally part of a theatrical backdrop.

RIGHT: This top-floor sitting room is the preserve of Cath's husband, the music producer Hugh Padgham.

OVERLEAF: A view from the telly room through one of its gothic windows to the garden beyond

ABOUT THE HOMEOWNERS

The Manor House

Joanna Wood is one of Britain's leading interior designers and the founder of an eponymous international interior design practice based in Belgravia, London. She is married to Charles Hansard and has two daughters.

The Thatched Cottage

Bee Osborn is a multi–award winning interior designer and founder of Studio Osborn, which works on both hotel and residential projects. Her company also designs furniture, lighting and home accessories.

The Columbarium

Amanda Hornby trained in fashion and textiles before moving into interior design twenty years ago. She lives in Hodges Barn with husband Nicholas and their three children. The house has been in Nicholas's family since 1945.

The Mason's House

Peruvian-born Tatiana Tarfur is co-founder of an eponymous design company producing handmade furniture and decorative surfaces for interiors. She and husband Lord Howard of Effingham live in the Cotswolds with their twin children.

The Old Rectory

Lesley Cooke is an acclaimed interior decorator and landscape designer who works on projects in both London and the countryside. Her photographs of life in the Cotswolds have won her a large following on Instagram.

The Hovel

James Mackie is a former senior director of Sotheby's and a much heralded interior decorator and art advisor. He lives at Muffities with his partner, the writer and gardener Arthur Parkinson.

The High House

Caroline Baker owns and runs an eponymous company specialising in property management for some of the highest-net-worth families in the world. She and daughter Tatiana divide their time between London and the Cotswolds.

The Farm Worker's Cottage

Alexandra Tolstoy is an Anglo-Russian adventurer, author, TV presenter and mother of three. She organises riding trips to Kyrgyztan and is the founder of the Tolstoy Edit, which sells antique furniture and textiles.

The Arts and Crafts House

Robin Smith Sulger was born in South Carolina and now lives in the Cotswolds with her husband, Justin, and their two daughters. She is the founder of Veld Studio, which specialises in interior renovations and design.

The Dovecote

Emma Burns is managing director of Sibyl Colefax and John Fowler, one of the UK's longest-established and most respected interior decorating firms. She lives in Bampton with her supremely elegant pug, Dahlia.

The Georgian Farmhouse

Vanessa Macdonald runs Melissa Wyndham Ltd., one of *House and Garden*'s leading interior design practices. She hails from the Americas but now lives the Cotswolds with her art consultant husband, James, and their two sons.

The Village House

Paul Tabor is a serial entrepreneur and CEO of the electric bike company Evari Bikes. He lives in Meysey Hampton Manor with his partner, the Danish artist Julie Gad, and their daughters.

The Hotchpotch

Sam and Georgie Pearman are celebrated publicans, hoteliers and restaurateurs with establishments in both the Cotswolds and London. Georgie is also an interior decorator and product designer. And Sam also makes beer.

Cottage Industry

Archie Mackie and his wife, Caddy, own a company selling vintage and industrial furniture and lighting alongside decorative antiques. Original House is based in Calmsden, in the heart of the Cotswolds.

The Stately Home

Sir Michael Bishop (now Baron Glendonbrook) is a prominent businessman, conservative peer and the previous owner of the airline BMI. He and his partner, property developer Martin Ritchie, bought Bruern Abbey in 2012.

Paradise

Designer Cath Kidston MBE set up a home furnishings and fashion business with more than two hundred eponymously named stores across the world. Her husband, Hugh Padgham, is a multi Grammy-winning record producer.

OPPOSITE: Fyfield Manor

ACKNOWLEDGEMENTS

Firstly, our thanks to all the owners who invited us into their homes and let us clank around with our equipment, fussily rearrange cushions, co-opt their children and dogs into the project, and generally make a nuisance of ourselves. They were all extremely gracious and generous with their time. Along the way we were treated to all manner of cocktails, cakes, and al fresco lunches. It was a delight to meet so many fabulous people and a privilege to be able to snoop round their houses.

We are extremely grateful to Edla Marlborough for so kindly agreeing to write the foreword and for welcoming us to Blenheim Palace.

Of course, in the process of researching the book we scouted countless beautiful houses which purely for reasons of space didn't end up on these pages, and we are indebted to their owners as well. We are also grateful to the many people who suggested houses, effected introductions, and encouraged us in our endeavours.

In particular, we would like to thank Christine Ansell-Wells, Lucy Abel-Smith, Emily Archer, Flora Astor, Ally Bailey, Jane Bigos, Leonora Birts, Anton Brech, Caroline Brown, Coco Campbell, John and Shellard Campbell, Pandora Cooper-Key, Tania Corbett, Laura de Ganay, Anna Dewar, Jessica Dickinson, Phoebe Dickinson, Mark Eastment, Laura Elgar, Daisy Finer, Peter Finer, Mark Fletcher, Katharina Florh, Clemmie Fraser, Sebastian Gibson, Jane Gordon, Joshua Hale, Ali Hope, Charlie Horton, Caryn Hibbert, Amanda Hodge, Jeff Holland, Pippa Hornby, Sam Keys, Elly James, Magdalen Jebb, Alexander Jones, Rachel Jones, Stephen Lewis, Toby Lorford, Ian Mitchell, Jenny Nicholson, Polly Oswald, Jorge Perez-Martin, Sally Rowland, Bex Sanchez, Beatrice Santell, Sophie Stevenson, Susannah Taylor, Paul Thomas, Joanna Thorpe, Suzanne Tise-Isore, Harold Van Lier, Bee Van Zuylen, Susan Wells, Victoria Wormsley, and Country House Supremo Lindsay Cuthill.

Finally, we would like to thank Shawna Mullen for her vision and guidance, and everybody else at Abrams who worked with us on Project "Catswolds," especially Peggy Garry and Darilyn Lowe Carnes.

INDEX

A
Alun-Jones, Deborah, 77
Amanpour, Christiane, 50
ancient Romans, 11, 12, 49, 104
Anglo-Saxons, 12
Anne (Queen), 7, 153
Area of Outstanding Natural Beauty (AONB), 7, 11
Arlington Row, *10*, 11
Armytage, Marcus, 115
Arts and Crafts House
    bedrooms, 136, *136*, 137, *137*
    drawing room, *134–35*, 135
    flagstoned front hall, 128, *128*
    front door, *126*, 127
    kitchen and dining room, 131, *132–33*
    landing, 136, *136*
    southern elevation, *130–31*, 131
    view from kitchen terrace, *138–39*, 139
Astor, Michael, 202
Austen, Jane, 77
Axelby, Sarah-Jane, 116
Aynhoe Park, 166

B
Baker, Caroline, 103–4, 232, *232*
Baker, Tatiana, 103
Bampton. *See* The Dovecote
Bateman, Charles Edward, 127
bathrooms
    Bee's Cottage, 44, *45*
    Bruern Abbey, 214, *214*
    The Dovecote, 146, *147*
    Farmhill Park, 184, *184*
    Fyfield Manor, 32, *33*
    High House, 107, *107*, 110, *111*
    Hodges Barn, 57, *57*, 58, *58*, 61, *61*
    Meysey Hampton Manor, 172, *172*
    Muffities, 98, *98*
    Old Rectory, 87, *87*
    Paradise, 218–19, 226, *227*
    Puffets, 75, *75*
    Tally Cottage, 194, *195*
    Whitehill Farmhouse, 161, *161*, 163, *163*
Battle of Blenheim, 153
bedrooms
    Arts and Crafts House, 136, *136*, 137, *137*
    Bee's Cottage, 44, *44*
    Bruern Abbey, *212–13*, 213, 214, *214*
    The Dovecote, 146, *146*
    Farmhill Park, 184, *184*
    farm worker's cottage, 116, 124, *124*
    Fyfield Manor, 32, *32*
    High House, 110, *110*, *111*
    Hodges Barn, 50, *56*, 57, *58*, *59*, *60–61*, 61, 62, *62*
    Meysey Hampton Manor, 172, *172*, *173*
    Muffities, 97, *97*
    Old Rectory, *86–87*, 87, *88*, 89, *89*
    Paradise, 226, *226–27*
    Tally Cottage, 194, *194*
    Whitehill Farmhouse, *160*, 161
beech wood, 15, *15*
Bee's Cottage (Old Post Office)
    bathroom, 44, *45*
    Blue Room, 38, 40, *40*
    boot room, 38, *38*
    dining table, 42, *42*
    kitchen, 42, *43*
    Love Shack, *46–47*, 47
    main bedroom, 44, *44*
    the snug (sitting room), 38, 40, *41*
    spare bedroom, 44, *44*
    in summer, 39, *39*
    in winter, *36–37*, 37
Belloc, Hilaire, 8
Betjeman, John, 77
Birts, Leonora, 103
Bishop, Michael (Lord Glendonbrook), 202–3, *233*, 233
Blenheim Palace, *6–7*, 7–8
    south façade, 8, *8*
books. *See* libraries and book rooms
boot room
    Bee's Cottage, 38, *38*
    Tally Cottage, 198, *198*
Bossom, Rosanna, 103
Bridget Jones's Diary (film), 11
van Brienen, Irene, 49
Brontë sisters, 77
Bronze Age, 128
Brooke, Rupert, 77
Bruern Abbey, 201–3
    bathroom, 214, *214*
    the Canal, 203, *204*
    courtyard, 203, *205*
    Gallery Hall, *206–7*, 207
    garden, 203, *205*
    guest bedroom, *212–13*, 213
    kitchen, 211, *211*
    media room, 214, *215*
    Music Room (sitting room), 208, *208–9*
    south façade, *200*, 201
    staircase, *210*, 211
    vaulted bedroom, 214, *214*
    view from drawing room, 203, *203*, 207, *207*
Buildings of England (Pevsner), 25
Bulmer, Edward, 92, 103
Burford, 13, *13*
Burns, Emma, 141–42, 232, *232*
Burns, Simon, 143

C
Carroll, Lewis, 77
Charles I (king), 217
Churchill, John (Duke of Marlborough), 7, 153
Church of St. Andrew, 17, *18–19*
Cider with Rosie (Lee), 217
Cistercian Abbey, 202
Colefax, Sibyl, 142
Collins, Angel, 203
columbaria. *See* Hodges Barn
Cooke, Lesley, 78, 232, *232*
Cope, John, 202
Corinium Dobunnorum, 104

cottages. *See* Bee's Cottage; farm worker's cottage; Tally Cottage
Coward, Noël, 201

D

Daylesfordshire, 17
Deer Park, of Great Barrington Park, *14–15*, 15
Diaz, Cameron, 37
dining rooms
    Arts and Crafts House, 131, *132–33*
    Farmhill Park, 186, *186*
    High House, 109, *109*
    Hodges Barn, 55, *55*
    Meysey Hampton Manor, 174, *174*
    Old Rectory, *82–83*, 83
    Paradise, 223, *223*
    Whitehill Farmhouse, 16, *162*
The Dovecote, 141–43, *145*, 151
    bathroom, 146, *147*
    book barn, 143, *143*
    drinks table, *150*, 151
    hall stairs, 142, *142*
    kitchen, 142, 144, *144*
    library, *148–49*, 149
    main bedroom, 146, *146*
    pigeonholes, *140*, 141
Downton Abbey (TV series), 11, 141
drawing rooms
    Arts and Crafts House, *134–35*, 135
    Bruern Abbey, view from, 203, *203*, 207, *207*
    Farmhill Park, 180, *180–81*
    Fyfield Manor, 25, *28*, 29
    Meysey Hampton Manor, 170, *170*
    Old Rectory, *84–85*, 85
    Paradise, 222, *222*
    Whitehill Farmhouse, *158–59*, 159
drinks tables
    The Dovecote, *150*, 151
    Farmhill Park, 186, *187*
    Paradise, 224, *224*

E

Eliot, George, 77
English Journey (Priestley), 65
en suite bathrooms
    Farmhill Park, 184, *184*
    Whitehill Farmhouse, 161, *161*
Extinction Rebellion, 178

F

façades
    Blenheim Palace, 8, *8*
    Bruern Abbey, *200*, 201
    Fyfield Manor, 24, *24*
    Meysey Hampton Manor, *164*, 165
    Old Rectory, *76*, 77
    Paradise, *216*, 217
    Whitehill Farmhouse, *152*, 153
Farmhill Park, 177–78, *178*
    bedroom, 184, *184*
    cabinet in hall, 184, *185*
    central bay, *176*, 177
    dining room, 186, *186*
    drawing room, 180, *180–81*
    drinks table, 186, *187*
    en suite bathroom, 184, *184*
    fireplace, 178, *179*
    kitchen, 182, *183*
    office, 182, *182*
    sideboard in, 186, *186*
farmhouse. *See* Whitehill farmhouse
farm worker's cottage
    AGA oven, 117, *117*
    children's bedroom, 116, 124, *124*
    cloakroom, 124, *125*
    garden path, *114*, 115
    kitchen, 116, *118–19*, 119
    main bedroom, 116, 124, *124*
    office, 124, *125*
    sitting room, *120–23*, 122
The Flower Yard (Raven), 92
Forest Green Rovers (football team), 178
Fowler, John, 142
Fyfield Manor
    drawing room, 25, *28*, 29
    façade of, 24, *24*
    gardens, 26, 34, *34–35*
    guest bedrooms in, 32, *32*
    kitchen, 26, *27*
    main bathroom, 32, *33*
    study, *30–31*, 31

G

Gad, Julie, 165–66, 233, *233*
gardens
    Bruern Abbey, 203, *205*
    farm worker's cottage, *114*, 115
    Fyfield Manor, 26, 34, *34–35*
    Muffities, 92, *92*
    Puffets, 67, *67*
Georgian farmhouse. *See* Whitehill Farmhouse
Glendonbrook, Lord (Michael Bishop), 202–3, 233, *233*
Great Barrington, 65
Great Barrington Park, *14–15*, 15
guest bedrooms
    Bruern Abbey, *212–13*, 213
    Fyfield Manor, 32, *32*
    Old Rectory, 89, *89*
    Tally Cottage, 194, *194*
Gypsy (dog), 29, *29*

H

Hansard, Charles, 25
Hare, Nick, 49
Haslam, Nicky, 218
Hemans, Felicia Dorothea, 201
Henry VIII (king), 202
High House, *102*, 103–4
    bathroom, 110, *111*
    bedrooms, 110, *110*, *111*
    desk, 113, *113*
    dining room, 109, *109*
    downstairs bathroom, 107, *107*
    hallway, 104, *104–5*
    kitchen, *108*, 109
    shepherd's hut, *112*, 113
    sitting room, *106–7*, 107
Hodges Barn, *48*, 49
    bathrooms, 57, *57*, 58, *58*, 61, *61*
    bedroom, 50, *56*, 57
    dining room, 55, *55*
    dormitory, 50, 62, *62–63*
    floating staircase, *54*, 55, *55*
    flower room, 53, *53*
    garden hall, 50, *51*
    hummingbird bedroom, 62, *62*
    kitchen, 50, *52*, 53
    main bedroom, *60–61*, 61
    pomegranate bedroom, 58, *59*
The Holiday (film), 37
Hornby, Amanda, 49–50, 231, *231*
Hornby, Nicholas, 49–50
hotchpotch. *See* Farmhill Park
"hovel." *See* Muffities

Howard, Tatiana, 65–66
hunting, 189

J
Johnston Cave, 26

K
Kidston, Cath, 217–19, 233, *233*
Kidston, Glen "Lucky," 218
kitchens
    Arts and Crafts House, 131, *132–33*
    Bee's Cottage, 42, *43*
    Bruern Abbey, 211, *211*
    The Dovecote, 142, 144, *144*
    Farmhill Park, 182, *183*
    farm worker's cottage, 116, *118–19*, 119
    Fyfield Manor, 26, *27*
    High House, *108*, 109
    Hodges Barn, 50, *52*, 53
    Meysey Hampton Manor, 174, *175*
    Muffities, *100–101*, 101
    Old Rectory, 78, 80, *80–81*
    Puffets, *70–71*, 71
    Tally Cottage, 190, 196, *196*, 198, *199*
    Whitehill Farmhouse, *162*, 163

L
Lancaster, Nancy, 26
The Lark Ascending (Williams), 167
Laurie Lee Country, 17
Law, Jude, 37
Lee, Laurie, 217
libraries and book rooms
    The Dovecote, 143, *143*, *148–49*, 149
    Meysey Hampton Manor, *168–69*, 169
    Muffities, 92, 93, *93*, 95
    Paradise, 224, *225*
limestone, 65
Little Barrington, 21, *21*, 64, 65, 66
Louis XIV (king), 7
Lower Whitehill Farm. *See* Whitehill Farmhouse
Lucky Onion group, 177

M
Macdonald, Vanessa, 153–54, 233, *233*
Mackie, Archie, 189–90, 233, *233*
Mackie, James, 91–93, 232, *232*
Marlborough, Duke of (John Churchill), 7, 153
Marlborough, Edla, 8, *9*

Massingham, H. J., 165
Melissa Wyndham Ltd, 154–55
Methuen, Lawrence, 49
Meyers, Nancy, 37
Meysey Hampton Manor, 165–67, *167*
    bathroom, 172, *172*
    bedroom, 172, *172*
    dining room, 174, *174*
    drawing room, 170, *170*
    kitchen, 174, *175*
    library, *168–69*, 169
    main bedroom, 172, *173*
    main façade, *164*, 165
    staircase, 170, *171*
    urn, 166, *166*
Midge (dog), 8, *9*
Miserden valley, 21, *21*
Moore, Charles, 77
Morris, William, 11, 127
Moss, Kate, 25
Mouse (dog), 8, *9*
Muffities, *90*, 91–93
    bar, 101, *101*
    bathroom, 98, *98*
    bedroom, 97, *97*
    Book Room, 92, 93, *93*, 95, *95*
    garden sunshade, 92, *92*
    kitchen, *100–101*, 101
    sitting room, 92, 98, *98–99*
Munch, Edvard, 93

N
No. 131 (hotel), 177
Northanger Abbey (Austen), 77

O
Old Post Office. *See* Bee's Cottage
Old Rectory
    bathroom, 87, *87*
    bedrooms, *88*, 89
    Blue Room, 89, *89*
    dining room, *82–83*, 83
    drawing room, *84–85*, 85
    façade, *76*, 77
    guest bedroom, 89, *89*
    kitchen, 78, 80, *80–81*
    main bedroom, *86–87*, 87
    pool, 78, *79*
    study, 78, 83, *83*

    terrace, 78, *79*
"The Old Vicarage, Grantchester" (Brooke), 77
Orr-Ewing, Archie, 203
Osborn, Bee, 37–38, 231, *231*

P
Paradise, 217–18, *219*
    bathroom, 218–19, 226, *227*
    bedrooms, 226, *226–27*
    dining room, 223, *223*
    drawing room, 222, *222*
    drinks table, 224, *224*
    front façade, *216*, 217
    front hall, *220–21*, 221
    library, 224, *225*
    painted table in entrance hall, 221, *221*
    sitting room, 228, *228–29*
    telly room, 223, *223*, 228, *230*
Parkinson, Arthur, 91–93
Pearman, Georgie, 177–78, 233, *233*
Pearman, Sam, 177–78, 233, *233*
Perkins, James, 166
Pevsner, 25, 65
The Pottery Gardener (Raven), 92
Pride and Prejudice (film), 11
Priestley, J. B., 65
Puffets, 64, 65–66, *68–69*
    bathroom, 75, *75*
    garden, 67, *67*
    hallway, 72, *72*
    kitchen, *70–71*, 71
    nursery floor, 73, *73*
    spice boxes, 67, *67*
    staircase, 74, *74*
    study, 71, *71*

R
Raven, Sarah, 92
Ritchie, Martin, 202–3, 233, *233*
River Windrush, 13, *13*
rock, 12
Romans, ancient, 11, 12, 49, 104
Royal Gloucestershire, 17
Royal Horticultural Society, 203

S
The Scream (Munch), 93
Shaw, George Bernard, 77

shed, Tally Cottage
    exterior, 190, *191*
    interior, *192*, 193, *193*
sheep, 12, *12*, 13
Sheep Street, Burford, 13, *13*
shepherd's hut, High House, *112*, 113
Sieff, Diana, 203
sitting rooms
    Bee's Cottage, 38, 40, *41*
    Bruern Abbey, 208, *208–9*
    farm worker's cottage, *120–23*, 122
    High House, *106–7*, 107
    Muffities, 92, 98, *98–99*
    Paradise, 228, *228–29*
    Tally Cottage, 196, *196–97*
Smith Sulgar, Robin, 127–28, 232, *232*
Snowshill. *See* Arts and Crafts House
Sotheby's, 91, 93
staircases
    Bruern Abbey, *210*, 211
    Hodges Barn, *54*, 55, *55*
    Meysey Hampton Manor, 170, *171*
    Puffets, 74, *74*
stately home. *See* Bruern Abbey
St. John the Baptist's Church, 13, *13*
stone walls, *16*, 17
Strong, Thomas, 65, 66

studies
    Fyfield Manor, *30–31*, 31
    Old Rectory, 78, 83, *83*
    Puffets, 71, *71*

T
Tabor, Paul, 165–66, 233, *233*
Tafur, Tatiana, 66, 231, *231*
Tally Cottage, *188*, 189–90
    bathroom, 194, *195*
    boot room, 198, *198*
    guest bedroom, 194, *194*
    kitchen, 190, 196, *196*
    kitchen terrace, 198, *199*
    shed (exterior), 190, *191*
    shed (interior), *192*, 193, *193*
    sitting room, 196, *196–97*
Tame, John, 12, 17
Tolstoy, Alexandra, 115–17, 232, *232*
Tolstoy, Leo, 116
Tolstoy, Nikolai, 116
Trollope, Anthony, 77

V
Vanbrugh, John, 7
Vaulx, James, 165
Verey, David, 25

Verity and Beverley (architectural firm), 49
village house. *See* Meysey Hampton Manor

W
War of the Spanish Succession, 153
Whitehill Farmhouse, *155*, *156–57*
    bathrooms, 161, *161*, 163, *163*
    bedroom, *160*, 161
    croquet lawn, 154, *154*
    dining room, *162*, 163
    drawing room, *158–59*, 159
    en suite bathroom, 161, *161*
    flagstoned front hall, 159, *159*, *162*, 163
    front façade, *152*, 153
    guest bathroom, 163, *163*
    guest cottage, 163, *163*
    kitchen, *162*, 163
Williams, Ralph Vaughan, 167
Winslet, Kate, 37
Wood, Joanna, 25–26, 231, *231*
wool, 12
wool churches, 12
Wren, Christopher, 65
Wyatt, Henry, 178
Wyndham, Melissa, 154–55

Editor: Shawna Mullen
Designer: Darilyn Lowe Carnes
Managing Editor: Lisa Silverman
Production Manager: Sarah Masterson Hally

Library of Congress Control Number: 2022932882

ISBN: 978-1-4197-5979-6
eISBN: 978-1-64700-588-7

Text copyright © 2022 Milo Campbell and Katy Campbell
Photographs copyright © 2022 Mark Nicholson

Cover © 2022 Abrams

Published in 2022 by Abrams, an imprint of ABRAMS. All rights reserved. No portion of this book may be reproduced, stored in a retrieval system, or transmitted in any form or by any means, mechanical, electronic, photocopying, recording, or otherwise, without written permission from the publisher.

Printed and bound in China
10 9 8 7 6 5 4 3 2 1

Abrams books are available at special discounts when purchased in quantity for premiums and promotions as well as fundraising or educational use. Special editions can also be created to specification. For details, contact specialsales@abramsbooks.com or the address below.

Abrams® is a registered trademark of Harry N. Abrams, Inc.

ABRAMS
The Art of Books

195 Broadway
New York, NY 10007
abramsbooks.com